CW00421631

To Penny & Robbie
with lots of love.

Terry x

"fork it!"

Christmas 2023.

WITHNAIL & I
FROM CULT TO CLASSIC

TOBY BENJAMIN

FOREWORD BY
BRUCE ROBINSON

TITAN BOOKS

ABOVE: Photo by Murray Close.

WITHNAIL & I: FROM CULT TO CLASSIC
ISBN (print): 9781803362397
ISBN (ebook): 9781803362427

Published by
Titan Books
A division of Titan Publishing Group Ltd
144 Southwark Street
London SE1 0UP

First edition: August 2023
10 9 8 7 6 5 4 3 2 1

© 2023 Toby Benjamin
Photos by Murray Close © Murray Close

Book design by Amazing 15

Did you enjoy this book? We love to hear from our readers. Please e-mail us at: readerfeedback@titanemail.com or write to Reader Feedback at the above address. To receive advance information, news, competitions, and exclusive offers online, please sign up for the Titan newsletter on our website: www.titanbooks.com

No part of this publication may be reproduced, stored in a retrieval system, or transmitted, in any form or by any means without the prior written permission of the publisher, nor be otherwise circulated in any form of binding or cover other than that in which it is published and without a similar condition being imposed on the subsequent purchaser.

A CIP catalogue record for this title is available from the British Library.

Printed and bound in China.

CONTENTS

Foreword by Bruce Robinson 4

Introduction by Toby Benjamin 6

CAST AND CREW

Bruce Robinson: The Screenwriter................... 10

Bruce Robinson 16

Richard E. Grant...................................... 30

Paul McGann 36

Ralph Brown 48

Daragh O'Malley 58

Michael Wardle 62

Sue Love 66

The Screenplay 74

The Soundtrack 82

Rick Wentworth 86

David Dundas 90

Peter Frampton 96

Murray Close 102

Anthony Wise 112

The Journey From Cult To Classic.............116

Matthew Binns.......................................126

Peter Hannan 138

Acknowledgements...............................144

THE AUDIENCE

Diane Morgan 54

Paul Tanter 57

Bernard Casey 61

James Ponsoldt 65

Andrew Birkin 69

Gerard Johnson 83

Matt Johnson..84

Margaret Cho..88

Martin Kessler 95

Alistair Barrie 98

Paul Webb 104

Charlie Higson 106

Dean Cameron 111

Iain Morris 114

Richard Fleury 124

Tim Ellis..135

Sam Bain 136

Steve Doherty 142

Donal Logue...143

BY BRUCE ROBINSON

I FEEL UNUSUAL

By definition the contributors to this book have more to say about Withnail than I do and I thank them all for saying it. I wrote the story in Camden Town in the winter of 1970, and can barely believe I'm still writing about it 52 years later. I couldn't afford a pickled onion in those long-gone Withnail days, couldn't imagine I would ever achieve my daft desire to be a writer.

Withnail is the beginning of that desire. 10 fags and a clapped-out Olivetti with a missing a-key, garbage wine and phone-boxes stinking of piss. It was written in lean times but inspired in a time of hope. None of this Global-Britain bollocks, in those days Britain was global by its existence and the world acknowledged our contribution to it. Nobody gave a fuck for rubbish like 'Brexit,' because we had The Beatles, nor troubled themselves with that confetti of platitudinous clap-trap called, 'Taking Back Control,' (actually a ruse by off-shore tax-evaders).

Well, now we've 'taken it back,' and British Airways is a Spanish Company, and Rolls Royce a German car. Thatcherism has sold-off everything England ever owned, and our country is up to its knees in shit.

When Uncle Monty said, "Shat on by Tories," I never imagined such a line could become a literal reality. I could never have imagined Withnail's, "Free to those that can afford it, very expensive to those that can't," would ever actually apply to this lamentable island of ours.

"I have of late," wrote the Boss, "lost all my mirth," and that's how I feel about his 'Sceptred Isle' and its imminent Karaoke Thatcher. What has happened to our country, where is England gone? How have we allowed a coterie of avaricious nonentities to turn it into a milk-cow in the sea.

B.R September 2022

'LISTEN, WE'RE BONA FIDE.'

THE WITHNAIL & I BOOK

INTRODUCTION BY TOBY BENJAMIN

BELOW: Bruce discusses dinner with Withnail and Marwood. Photo by Murray Close.

OPPOSITE: Marwood and Withnail up on them moors. Photo by Murray Close.

'**A**h, my boys, my boys, we're at the end of an age. We live in a land of weather forecasts and breakfasts that 'set in'. Shat on by Tories. Shovelled up by Labour. And here we are. We three. Perhaps the last island of beauty in the world.'

I first watched this timeless, incredibly funny yet heart-breaking film thirty years ago, and it feels more relevant than ever today. I've obsessed over the film for decades, read everything I could about it, but felt I had yet to get to its true essence and wanted to know what it was like being a part of the film – how it felt to be there.

Seven years ago, I went to a gig in Brighton and as the hall was filling up, I saw Paul McGann heading ever nearer, peering at his ticket until he sat down right next to me.

I'd wanted to write a book about *Withnail & I* with Bruce Robinson for a decade, but had never been able to get in contact with him. I asked Paul if he thought Bruce would ever agree to

work on a book about the film. He shook his head.

'Not in a million years.'

In the middle of lockdown, I gave it one more go and wrote to Bruce. As luck would have it, I received a hand-written letter back saying he was getting bored of shooting slugs in his garden and that he'd be up for an interview.

Bruce invited me to a delightful weekend in the country, where I scanned the incredible memorabilia now published in this book for the first time. I am honoured that Bruce has written a foreword.

In his interview, we discussed how he found the funding, the casting with Mary Selway, David Dundas' and Rick Wentworth's soundtrack, Peter Hannan's cinematography, the comedy that has no jokes, the sets and locations, his cultural inspiration, the politics of the film and their parallels in our post-Brexit world. We discussed how he overcame the conflict with HandMade that almost shut the film down on day one, and how he drilled the cast line by line, so that his script remained fully intact in the film.

Bruce introduced me to his dear friend Andrew Birkin, who was instrumental in getting George Harrison at HandMade films a copy of Bruce's original script. Andrew offered great insights about the film's development, explained how Bruce's character was reflected in the cast, and even revealed how he types up his dialogue.

Bruce also intro'd me to David Dundas, his Camden landlord back in those halcyon days of '69 and the composer of the film's soundtrack. I discussed with David how he had to try to recreate the music that was inside Bruce's head, and how it took shape in his home studio on a four-track that had previously been used in recording *The Wall* by Roger Waters.

It was wonderful to interview David's co-composer Rick Wentworth about those fascinating creative moments as *Withnail's* theme emerged. Rock writer Neil Ferguson delves further into their work on the soundtrack and how it worked as a counterbalance to the heavyweight '60s tracks.

ABOVE: 'Two large gins, two pints of cider. Ice in the cider.' The King Henry location, Stony Stratford. Photo by Murray Close.

Classic car specialist Richard Fleury writes of the other stars of the film – the cars – and how Bruce's own decrepit Jag had a run-in with a tractor.

I tracked down Tony Wise, the actor who told Withnail to 'Get in the back of the van', and gentle Daragh O'Malley who played the Irishman with such menace. I also spoke to the farmer Michael Wardle about randy bulls, antiquated tractors and how having his leg bound in polythene nearly put an end to his acting career.

I interviewed the official set photographer, Murray Close, whose wonderful photos – some of which have never been seen before, let alone published – enrich this book throughout. Murray squeezed into cramped spaces to document pivotal scenes and somehow created photos of astounding quality which visually deepen our reminiscences..

The film's makeup artist Peter Frampton talked about transforming Ralph into Danny, and giving Withnail the look of a four-day hangover. I talked to film hairdresser Sue Love about Monty's '30s look and why the hair and makeup trailer was the place to be.

In an enlightening interview with Ralph Brown, we discussed Bruce's incredible dialogue, how he talked down Marwood when he got the fear, and reprising his role of Danny for *Wayne's World 2*.

In Paul McGann's genuinely profound interview, we talked about the confusion of his casting, playing Bruce in the film, the dynamism between the two leads, crashing the Jag, Bruce's exacting direction and the excitement of being debut film actors on location.

Getting an interview with Richard E. Grant, who gave the performance of his life as Withnail, was the final piece in the jigsaw. He touched upon the auditions, how familiar it felt acting the role of an unemployed actor, Withnail's mania, what Bruce taught him about comedy, and his tragic recital of *Hamlet*'s soliloquy.

Richard Griffiths' portrayal of Uncle Monty generated such warm nostalgia from all the cast and crew that I interviewed. The love and respect his fellow actors still hold for him is remarkable.

I talked to Unit Production Manager location scout Matthew Binns about his incredible search for Crow Crag, and how he found Sleddale Hall, which is now owned by Tim Ellis, who I chatted to

> **"Working on this book, it became clear that Bruce Robinson stamped his personality all over *Withnail & I*, which has undoubtedly earned the right to be called a classic."**

about the recent renovations to the house.

Peter Hannan discussed how he shot the film with Bruce and Bob Smith, from the spectacular lighting as Paul McGann gets up from his chair in the opening scene in London right through to capturing rain-sodden Cumbria.

No greater indication of the importance of a film can be found than in the inspiration and influence upon future generations. This book features contributions from actors, directors and other creatives who have been influenced by *Withnail & I*, revealing their own *Withnail* story and what they love about the film. Charlie Higson's incredible piece about the *Withnail* script became a fascinating chapter of its own.

It was the film's audience that helped to keep this slow-burning classic alive as it gained cult status, and I felt it was vital that *Withnail* fans had a voice in this book.

Writer and journalist Martin Keady has written numerous articles on *Withnail & I*, and here writes essays that focus on the script and consider the journey that the film has taken from cult to classic, surviving the boozy flirtation with '90s lad culture. We have

witnessed the film's remarkable journey, from one that students watched (and drank along with) on video to a staple entry in any Best of British film list.

Withnail & I is Bruce Robinson's original and unique story of his friendship with Viv MacKerrell and his other flatmates who lived in David Dundas's Camden house.

This book has given Bruce and many of his cast and crew a timely opportunity for a deep retrospective that evokes the halcyon days of working on this film, which for many of them was an absolute highlight of their career.

Working on this book, it became clear that Bruce Robinson stamped his personality all over *Withnail & I*, which has undoubtedly earned the right to be called a classic. This project has given me a chance to revisit every detail, with an ever greater appreciation of what an incredible combination of perception, artistry, energy, devotion and sheer luck Bruce had in this gathering of talent at one unique moment in time.

So… 'Change down, man, find your neutral space. You got a rush. It will pass. Be seated.'

ABOVE LEFT: Bruce directing a lunch. Peter Kohn to rear of Sally Jones (continuity supervisor). Sally Jones passed away 1st of January 2009. Photo by Murray Close.

ABOVE RIGHT: Paul McGann with Sue Love (hairdresser) and Andrea Galer (costume designer).

BRUCE ROBINSON

THE SCREENWRITER

BY MARTIN KEADY

It is surely telling that *Withnail & I*, one of the greatest screenplays ever written, began existence not as a screenplay at all, but as a novel, because it proves that Bruce Robinson is primarily a writer-screenwriter rather than a writer-director, as he was on *Withnail & I*. Indeed, after his spectacular early success in cinema with his first two screenplays, *The Killing Fields* and *Withnail & I*, eventually began to ebb away, he returned to writing things other than screenplays, in particular his two late, great literary works: *The Peculiar Memories of Thomas Penman* (1998), a very thinly veiled autobiography; and *They All Love Jack: Busting the Ripper* (2015), his extraordinary attempt to establish definitively the true identity of Jack the Ripper. Ultimately, the screenplay for *Withnail & I* and those two books constitute what might be called 'The Bruce Robinson Trilogy', a trio of works that are his enduring legacy as a writer.

Bruce Robinson was born on 2nd May 1946 in London, less than a year after the end of WW2. Thus he was part of the remarkable generation of post-war children who would grow up to be the writers, artists and musicians who would transform Britain's image of itself and its image in the rest of the world from the 1960s onwards. Indeed, a direct comparison can be made with one of those other luminaries, Pete Townshend of The Who, because, just like Townshend, Robinson suffered an abusive childhood. His real father was Carl Casriel, an American lawyer with whom his mother, Mabel Robinson, had a short-lived affair during the war, a 'back-story' remarkably similar to that of Townshend's first great masterpiece, the rock-opera *Tommy*. Robinson's stepfather, Rob, an ex-RAF man, knew that Bruce was not his biological son and never let him forget it, subjecting him to appalling physical and psychological abuse. As Robinson said in an interview for this book: 'I had an unpleasant childhood, and consequently no education'.

Just as Pete Townshend would draw on his own memories of childhood confusion and suffering to create *Tommy*, so Robinson's creative life was fuelled by his stepfather's mistreatment of him. He wrote about it most directly in *The Peculiar Memories of Thomas Penman*, but arguably it was an influence on much of his other great writing, including *Withnail & I*. In that respect, Robinson proves the truth of Ernest Hemingway's famous adage that to be a writer you need two things above all: 'a cast-iron bullshit detector, and an unhappy childhood'.

Robinson grew up in Broadstairs, in Kent, and attended the Charles Dickens Secondary Modern School. This was fitting, because despite the obvious influence of Shakespeare on his writing, particularly in *Withnail & I*, it was Dickens who was his first literary love. As he told us in an interview for this book: 'When he [Dickens] is flying – at his best, no one's as good. I mean, *A Christmas Carol*, if he'd written just that it still would have been a gigantic career.' This comment is perhaps especially illuminating, as much the same could be said of Robinson himself: if he had only ever written *Withnail & I*, his would still have been 'a gigantic career'.

Nevertheless, for all his love of Dickens, Robinson's first creative outlet was not writing but acting. He was an undeniably beautiful young man, which certainly would not have hindered him in securing a place at the Central School of Speech and Drama in London. There, he would meet Vivian MacKerrell, the original inspiration for Withnail, and other lifelong friends who he would later collaborate with on *Withnail & I*, notably its composer David Dundas.

Almost immediately upon graduating from Central, Robinson's good looks, even more than his acting ability, won him a part in a major film, Franco Zeffirelli's *Romeo and Juliet* (1968). Unlike in previous stage or screen productions of the play, Zeffirelli was determined to use young actors to tell the ultimate tale of young love being first doomed and then destroyed by

old prejudices. This extraordinarily simple but effective casting decision was one of the major reasons for the film's enormous commercial and critical success. Indeed, Whiting and Hussey briefly became the unlikely poster-boy and poster-girl for the sexual revolution sweeping the Western world by the end of the 1960s. However, as befits one of Shakespeare's greatest tragedies, there was a darker, even unseemly side, to the movie, one that was instrumental in Robinson's development, first as an actor and then as a writer.

Zeffirelli was attracted to Robinson and at times expressed his sexual interest in him. Like so many other young actors in the film, the young Robinson was almost a modern-day equivalent of the exquisite and delicate young men immortalised in so many Renaissance paintings. However, he was also heterosexual. Moreover, Zeffirelli was not only much older (he was 45 when he filmed *Romeo and Juliet*) but, as the film's director, far more powerful than Robinson, an actor making his first movie. For Robinson, it was as if the play's overarching theme – of tender, impressionable youth being threatened and finally overwhelmed by the forces of age and entrenched financial power – was being brought menacingly to life.

In the post-#METOO era that we are now in, when women in the film industry in particular and in the world in general

ABOVE: Bruce and 'I'. Photo by Murray Close.

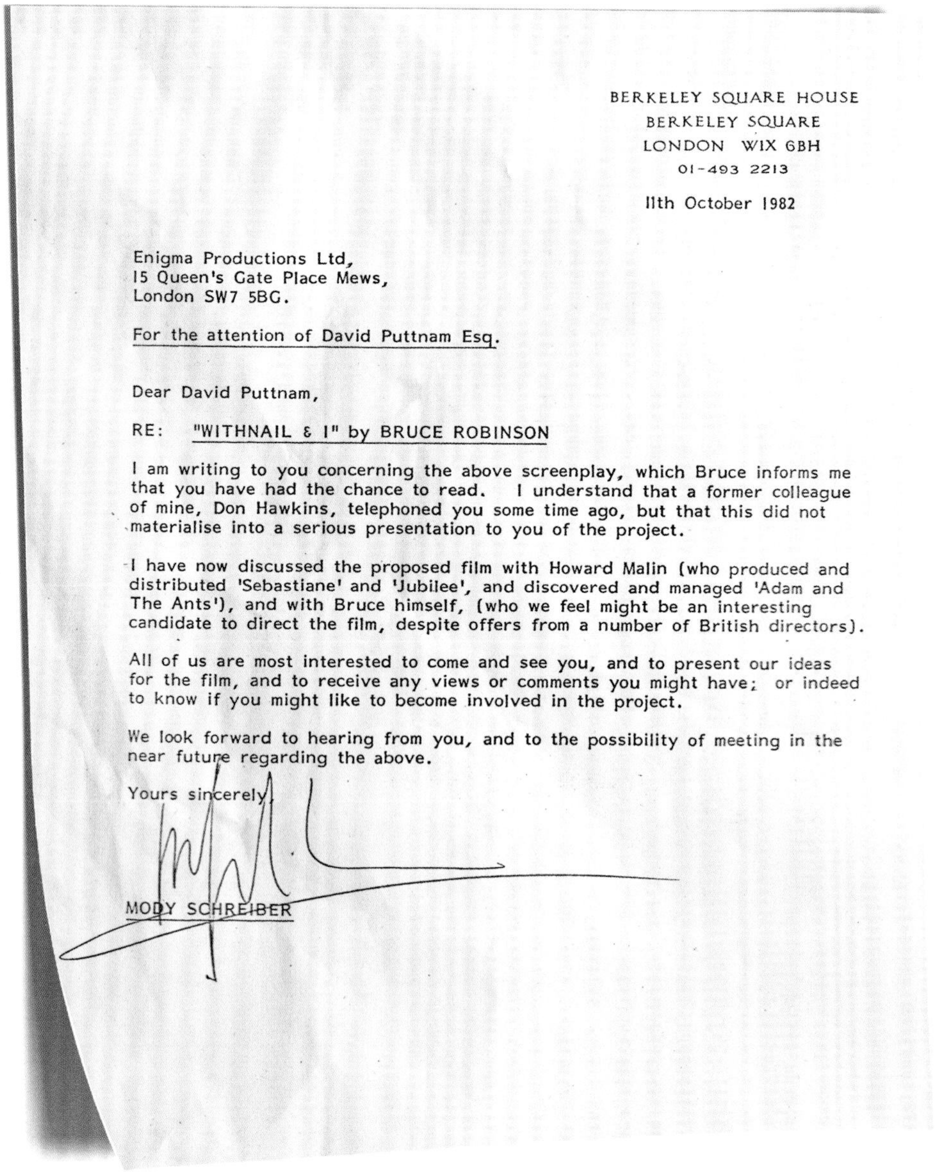

BERKELEY SQUARE HOUSE
BERKELEY SQUARE
LONDON W1X 6BH
01-493 2213

11th October 1982

Enigma Productions Ltd,
15 Queen's Gate Place Mews,
London SW7 5BG.

For the attention of David Puttnam Esq.

Dear David Puttnam,

RE: "WITHNAIL & I" by BRUCE ROBINSON

I am writing to you concerning the above screenplay, which Bruce informs me
that you have had the chance to read.   I understand that a former colleague
of mine, Don Hawkins, telephoned you some time ago, but that this did not
materialise into a serious presentation to you of the project.

I have now discussed the proposed film with Howard Malin (who produced and
distributed 'Sebastiane' and 'Jubilee', and discovered and managed 'Adam and
The Ants'), and with Bruce himself, (who we feel might be an interesting
candidate to direct the film, despite offers from a number of British directors).

All of us are most interested to come and see you, and to present our ideas
for the film, and to receive any views or comments you might have; or indeed
to know if you might like to become involved in the project.

We look forward to hearing from you, and to the possibility of meeting in the
near future regarding the above.

Yours sincerely

MODY SCHREIBER

of the next decade, Robinson worked mainly as a screen actor, including in films such as Ken Russell's *The Music Lovers* (1971), a biopic of Tchaikovsky, and *The Story of Adele H.* (1975), François Truffaut's film about the daughter of Victor Hugo.

However, Robinson's acting career did not all unfold on the sets of great directors such as Truffaut. Like almost all actors, there were long periods of 'resting', or unemployment, and even the odd foray into 'adult', or rather pornographic, movies. One example was *Kleinhoff Hotel* (1977), for which Robinson's face was on the poster (as one of the leads) but still very much in the background, as the main image was that of a naked woman in jackboots.

So, nearly a decade after graduating from drama school and walking almost immediately onto the set of *Romeo and Juliet*, Robinson found himself both struggling for work and struggling to maintain the boyish good looks that had been so much a part of his arsenal as an actor. Consequently, he found himself descending further and further into what might be called '*Withnail*-World', the demi-monde of talented but apparently unemployable actors that he would eventually immortalise in *Withnail & I*.

As a result, Robinson found himself turning to writing, or, more accurately, returning to it, because at the end of the 1960s he had produced the first draft of the original novel-version of *Withnail & I*. By the end of the 1970s, as his acting career began to draw to a close, he was increasingly interested in writing his own scripts rather than just learning those of others. He was encouraged when Mody Schreiber, a relatively little-known English film producer, paid him to adapt the original novel of *Withnail & I* into a screenplay. Then he came to the attention

are finally being listened to when they tell their stories of harassment and even assault, it is worth remembering that occasionally young men, such as Robinson, also found themselves being too closely observed, on and off set, by those with more power than them. For Robinson, it must have been doubly galling, as he had just escaped one abusive relationship at home with his stepfather before finding himself being thrust into another in his first real experience of work. Eventually, all these abuses and abusers of power would find themselves crystallised in the over-large form of Uncle Monty in *Withnail & I*, another elderly would-be predator who attempts to prey, almost vampirically, upon the young.

Despite Robinson's decidedly mixed experience of making the film, Zeffirelli's *Romeo and Juliet* was a huge hit, the most commercially successful film of a Shakespeare play ever made up to that point. Indeed, it was not just a commercial success but a cultural sensation, as it came to symbolise, like so much of the art of the Sixties (above all, of course, its pop music), the attempts of the world's youth to escape the dead but controlling hand of their parents. As a result, its cast, including Robinson, found themselves much in demand for other films. So, for much

ABOVE: Letter from Mody Schreiber to David Puttnam.

ABOVE RIGHT: Bruce at Sleddale Hall, July '86. Photo by Sophie Robinson.

" **His first two screenplays, for *The Killing Fields* and *Withnail & I*, are perhaps the finest two screenplays that anyone has ever written in succession.** "

of David Puttnam, who was the highest-profile British film producer of the time, including of masterpieces such as *Chariots of Fire* (1981) and *Local Hero* (1982).

After those successes, Puttnam was able to start making films that did not have just a British setting or subject matter, beginning with *The Killing Fields*, a film about Pol Pot's Cambodian genocide in the late 1970s. And Puttnam took Bruce Robinson with him, commissioning him, largely on the basis of his unfilmed *Withnail & I* screenplay, to adapt for the screen *The Death and Life of Dith Pran*, by Sydney Schanberg, a remarkable article for *The New York Times Magazine*. Schanberg was a Pulitzer Prize-winning writer whose most famous work was this account of his experiences in Cambodia, which was made possible by the assistance of a Cambodian fixer-turned-journalist, Dith Pran, who was himself captured and nearly killed by Pol Pot's legion of goons.

This was Robinson's second big break, and his first as a writer, after his initial break as an actor when he was hired for *Romeo and Juliet*. Schanberg's article had generated considerable interest from film producers, so it was almost bewildering that Puttnam hired a then-unknown writer to adapt it for the screen. And yet Puttnam, who had identified and then helped steer so many of the great British screenwriters and film directors of the 1980s, including Hugh Hudson and Bill Forsyth (the directors of *Chariots of Fire* and *Local Hero* respectively), must also have seen something in Robinson that convinced him he could write a great script. And that instinct was triumphantly vindicated when Robinson took what was already remarkable source material and turned it into an even more remarkable film, *The Killing Fields* (1984).

The Killing Fields was that rarest of things – an instant classic. Robinson's script, drawing on Schanberg's article but then adding his own unique wit and ear for dialogue (which had obviously been honed by his training and then working as an actor), was nominated for Best Adapted Screenplay. Although he lost out to Peter Shaffer, for Shaffer's own adaptation of his play *Amadeus*, he had still joined the lofty ranks of first-time

screenwriters whose scripts are nominated for an Oscar®.

The incredible success of *The Killing Fields* opened many doors for Robinson as a screenwriter. However, he had obviously learned something from his failure to capitalise on his initial success as an actor in *Romeo and Juliet*. So, rather than writing scripts for others, he set out to write (or rather rewrite, having already written the original novel and the first draft of the screenplay based upon it) a film about his own personal experiences of '*Withnail*-World': *Withnail & I*.

Arguably, only *Casablanca* matches the sheer 'memorability', or quotability, of *Withnail & I*, in that *every single line* of the screenplay is superb, a fact attested to not only by critics and fans but by those who first read it. Robinson had obviously lived the life depicted in the script and so he wrote about it with unflinching authenticity. And despite not originally having considered that he would direct it himself (he had never even directed a stage production up to that point), he was eventually convinced by Paul Heller, the producer of the film, that *only* he could direct it. The result, like *Casablanca*, is one of the few virtually *perfect* films ever made, in which every element of the film – including the acting, the direction and the score, which

ABOVE: Bruce Robinson (right) with producer Paul Heller (left) and associate producer Lawrence Kirstein (middle). Paul Heller passed away 28th of December 2020.

ABOVE: Bruce and camera operator Bob Smith shooting in London. Bob Smith passed away 25th of June 2012. Photo by Murray Close.

also liberally used classic 60s tracks – is almost flawless.

What may have begun in the late 1980s as a student drinking game, in which young men tried to keep up with the film's leads drink for drink while reciting its dialogue, gradually became a truly multi-generational phenomenon, whereby Sixties survivors could relive their lost youth and younger viewers could simultaneously marvel at and be appalled by the often grey and crushing reality, including worklessness, of life in that decade for those who were outside the small 'inner circle' of pop stars, photographers and film-makers.

However, for all its brilliance, *Withnail & I* was not immediately a hit on the scale of *Romeo and Juliet* or *The Killing Fields*. Instead, it became the very definition of a 'cult' or 'sleeper' hit, whereby it found a second and ultimately eternal life after its initial cinematic release, first on video, then on DVD and now on streaming services around the world. Indeed, for all the splendour of its cinematography by Peter Hannan, which made the Lake District look both more beautiful and more foreboding than at any time

since Wordsworth, the subtleties and sheer 'quotability' of the script arguably lent themselves even more to the kind of repeat viewing offered by smaller and cheaper screens. As a result, *Withnail & I* has itself become a kind of cinematic *rite de passage*, but one that must be taken and retaken at different periods of someone's life: from student-dom and the insane imbibing that Withnail and Marwood indulge in; to the reality of post-student working life, with all the impoverishment and petty humiliations that Withnail in particular rails at; through, perhaps, to middle and even late age, in the form of Uncle Monty.

All of the characterisation in *Withnail & I* is sublime. However, Robinson's greatest creation, even more than Withnail and Marwood, is arguably Uncle Monty. He starts off by portraying him as an obviously ridiculous figure of fun, ripe for the kind of exploitation (or at least the borrowing of his holiday cottage) that Withnail specialises in. Then, Robinson reveals him to be a more sinister, even decadent, figure, capable of rape (or 'burglary', as he puts it). Finally, and effectively before our eyes, he becomes an old

man, whose absence is almost mourned for the rest of the film, or at least for the following morning, when Withnail mocks the note that he leaves and Marwood expresses sympathy for 'the poor old bugger'. When one bears in mind the abuse that Robinson himself had suffered at the hands of his own abusers or would-be abusers – his stepfather and Zeffirelli – it is astonishing that he should finally make Uncle Monty such a sympathetic, even pitiable, figure.

The Killing Fields and *Withnail & I* are the 'twin peaks', or perhaps the classic one-two punch, of Robinson's screenwriting career – and most screenwriters only get to deliver such a classic pairing later in their career, rather than at the start of it. Therefore, it was almost inevitable that his cinematic career would go downhill thereafter. That is not to say that he did not write or direct other interesting, even fascinating, films, such as *Fat Man and Little Boy* (1989), his meticulously researched account of the Manhattan Project. However, there is really nothing, not even *The Rum Diary* (2011), his return to directing after years away to film an early Hunter S. Thompson novel, that genuinely bears comparison with *The Killing Fields* or *Withnail & I*.

Indeed, for a time Robinson almost became the living proof of the famous maxim of William Goldman, the great screenwriter and screenwriting guru, that screenwriters should never *just* be screenwriters, because otherwise the frustration of writing scripts that never get made will drive them mad. As Robinson put it in an interview for this book: 'I've written 40 screenplays and so few of them have been done'.

Fortunately for Robinson and his fans, it was as if he eventually realised the truth of Goldman's maxim and returned to writing things other than screenplays. Indeed, his non-screenwriting output has been remarkably varied, encompassing everything from children's books, such as *The Obvious Elephant* (2000) and *Harold and the Duck* (2005), both of which were illustrated by his wife, Sophie Windham, to the long-rumoured stage adaptation of *Withnail & I*, which will include material cut from the original film, such as the famous 'fencing' scene, during which Withnail continues to smoke incessantly despite wearing a fencing mask.

Nevertheless, there are two works in Robinson's later literary output that stand out above all the others.

First, having referred to it obliquely in much of his writing, including in *Withnail & I*, he explicitly drew upon his own troubled childhood in his 'fictionalised autobiography', *The Peculiar Memories of Thomas Penman* (1998). The key line, which is almost the tagline for the whole book, is: 'I was brought up like vomit'. For a long time, *Penman* was the only other creative work of his that Robinson ranked alongside *Withnail & I*, and it is easy to see why, as it brilliantly recreates the post-war period, when children like him seemed to have all the psychic trauma caused by WW2 visited upon them personally.

Secondly, Robinson took another typically left-field turn to write a comprehensively researched book (for a supposed sybarite, he has a formidable work ethic), which was his non-fiction epic, *They All Love Jack: Busting the Ripper* (2015), convincingly claiming to have revealed the true identity of the world's first world-famous serial killer.

Now in his mid-70s, but still looking ridiculously good for his age, Bruce Robinson is ultimately so much more than 'just' the writer-director of *Withnail & I*, just as his own literary hero, Charles Dickens, is so much more than 'just' the writer of his own best-known work, *A Christmas Carol*. Robinson has proved himself to be a superb writer in several distinct fields: autobiography, or at least 'fictional autobiography'; historical non-fiction; and screenwriting. His first two screenplays, for *The Killing Fields* and *Withnail & I*, are perhaps the finest two screenplays that *anyone* has ever written in succession. And if he has never quite matched them since, well, to quote Joseph Heller on his own early masterpiece *Catch-22*, nobody else has either.

ABOVE: Bruce with producer Paul Heller and Jag.

BRUCE ROBINSON
SCREENWRITER AND DIRECTOR

Withnail & I **came out quite a long time ago…**

It's amazing that it's sustained. It has an ingredient that was certainly not invented or intended by me that seems to be timeless.

What was it about King Curtis's 'A Whiter Shade of Pale' that created the right feeling for you for the opening scene?

I was having a drink round a friend's house and we were talking about the saxophone in jazz, and he put it on. I remember saying that if ever I make *Withnail & I*, that's in it.

A lot of the music in *Withnail* was like that. 'Hang out the Stars in Indiana' by the great Al Bowlly – someone I absolutely adored. All of those songs in *Withnail* were chosen after I'd written the novel but preceded the actual film. It was music that I had in my head around that period.

When you began writing *Withnail & I*, how many of the characters were in your mind at the start and how many appeared as you were writing?

The only characters in it initially are suggested by the title – *Withnail & I*. I knew there was going to be an Uncle Monty, but there weren't any others. There was the kebab seller down the road in Delancey Street, there was quite a bit about him and his wife – a midget with a wart with a hair growing out of it. There were people like that in the book, but that got reduced down to basically *Withnail & I* and their enemies, and who are their enemies? Everyone, and everyone attacks them. The farmer, the poacher, the Irishman, the cops, the scrubbers, everyone attacked them, because that's how I perceived life in those days, living on four quid national assistance.

Did you act the characters' voices out loud as you typed?

Absolutely, all I've ever written is done like that. I speak the characters' words and listen to them. I'll go off into the character, talking nonsense. I'll carry on until a line comes out of the mess

OPPOSITE: Covering letter from Bruce Robinson to Paul Heller, to accompany the script.

that will have some relevance: 'I'm going to pull your head off because I don't like your head,' and I'll think, that's not a bad line, I'll put that in, and another line will develop out of it and it's always been like that.

How crucial was David Puttnam's involvement in the film's development?

Before it was even a film script, one of my oldest friends, Andrew Birkin, was working for David and he'd written something that was going to be made. Andrew read the *Withnail & I* novel and gave it to Puttnam, and told him it had really made him laugh. Puttnam didn't care for it, but agreed I could write. So, about a year after that, Puttnam got hold of me and asked me to write a script for him, for which he paid 1,500 quid, and that was my first-ever cheque as a writer, except for fuck magazines like *Penthouse*. They used to give you a tenner to write letters for the wankers… 'Me and my girlfriend went down to Brighton…' etc…

I wrote a script for Puttnam called *The Silver Palace*, which was a comedy for children that didn't get made. He hired me (God bless him), two or three times to write scripts for him that weren't filmed, until one that was. The fact that *The Killing Fields* got made gave me enough credibility to make *Withnail*.

Who commissioned Ralph Steadman to draw the *Withnail & I* poster?

Don Hawkins, who was an actor friend of mine, was instrumental in this, and should have had a 'thank you' credit at the end of the movie, but didn't get one by default not design. Don gave a copy of the screenplay to his friend Mody Schreiber, who was very sweet and very rich – at least compared with the rest of us. Mody read it and came up with 3,000 quid to turn it into a screenplay. Once I wrote that, Don got hold of Steadman and we went down to ask him if he would do a drawing for it. The reason being, he did those drawings for *Fear and Loathing,* and we thought that *Withnail* was sort of an English *Fear and Loathing,* or at least was in that arena.

£9:756 := up to 30th June.

155:

77, Melrose Avenue,
Wimbledon Park,
London S.W.I9.

Paul Heller, Esq.,
I666, Beverley Drive,
Los Angeles, Calif.

RECEIVED 2 1 MAY 198?

My Dear Paul,

          here is my morbid little autobiography. In
case it amuses not, I'd like it known that it's a comedy,
and essentially very English. Some of it is a little difficult to understand, there's a lot of English slang in here,
(i.e. "Give us a tanner and I'll give him a bell" - trans-
lates as "Give me sixpence and I'll telephone him" etc), if
it hasn't grabbed by page ten I reccomend the trash can. I
would shoot it not unlike a modern "Gold Rush," bearing in
mind this is itself a period piece.

          We sent Michael North throbbing with curry -
had a nice evening with him & he seems to be enjoying himself.

          Hope you are in good spirits, and that you
find something to grin over in the script.

                    With all best wishes,

                    Bruce

                    Bruce Robinson.

ABOVE: Bruce fifteen
foot up on a cobra crane.
Photo by Murray Close.

How adept was Mary Selway at helping bring about your vision regarding the cast?

Mary was brilliant. Before I knew anything about the process. I naively thought: 'Who needs a casting director?' But because that's what she did, she was aware of every actor in the game. She was showing me photographs of young unknowns because we couldn't afford any names. Daniel Day-Lewis turned it down. She sent me this photograph, which I described at the time as a porky, young Dirk Bogarde, and that was Richard E. 'Christ, Mary! I want Byron's ghost to play this.' But Mary said: 'I think Richard has enough acidity to do it, will you see him?' I said no, but in her wisdom she over-rode that, and Richard did come in and he got the part.

Why do you think Bob Dylan's lyrics to 'All Along the Watchtower' as they left Camden were ideal?

That whole Camden Town period of my life was all about cheap red and getting smashed on 'pot' as it was then known. Perhaps one of the reasons the film survives is that nothing changes – people are still doing that, although no longer in Camden Town – all the wankers' caffs have acquired an 'e' at the end.

It was all about holes in your fucking shoes, and just about scraping enough for a bottle of red and a joint. Intense friendship. Intense laughter. The laughter got so bad you had to crawl out of the room to escape. I literally remember crawling across the floor with someone shooting another arrow of mirth into your side and just fucking collapsing flat on your face with laughter.

How did George Harrison get involved in the film?

It's strange the family tree of what happened with *Withnail*. I went to Los Angeles with Puttnam, who took me out to write a script for him. My girlfriend at that time, Lesley, came to LA and introduced me to this producer called Paul Heller, who sadly died recently.

Paul ended up producing *Withnail & I*, but at the start he thought I was a wanker hanging on to Lesley-Anne Down, who was an up-and-coming star in *Upstairs Downstairs*. He thought I was Mr. Anne Down.

Then Paul read something that I'd written and I remember him saying: 'I thought you were a dilettante; I didn't realise you could actually write.'

Then, *The Killing Fields* came out, and I had this *Withnail & I* script, and I said: 'God, I wish I could just find a way to get this

> ## " It was all about holes in your fucking shoes, and just about scraping enough for a bottle of red and a joint. "

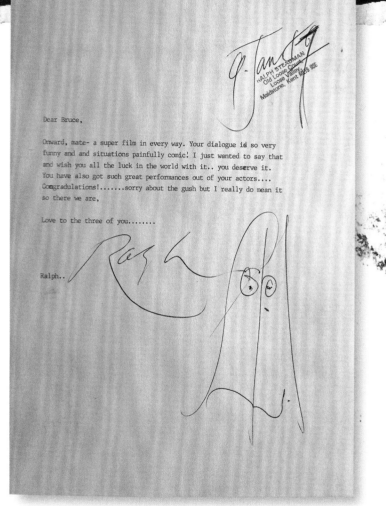

Dear Bruce,

Onward, mate- a super film in every way. Your dialogue id so very funny and and situations painfully comic! I just wanted to say that and wish you all the luck in the world with it.. you deserve it. You have also got such great performances out of your actors.... Congradulations!.......sorry about the gush but I really do mean it so there we are,

Love to the three of you........

Ralph..

made, and find a fucking director for it.' And he said: 'Why don't you direct it?

'It hasn't even crossed my mind, Paul.' (And God's honour, that was the truth.)

'If I get you the money, will you direct it?'

I recently found a photograph of Paul Heller, myself, and this guy called Larry Kirstein together in Ireland in front of an Irish post office called Hollywood Post Office, and we were sort of laughing about it. Anyway, Mr. Kirstein came up with half the dough.

Thereafter, a friend of mine, David Wimbury, got it into HandMade Films. It was read by Ray Cooper, a producer, and absent friend, who is also the percussionist for Elton John.

So, Ray loved it, Wimbury loved it, and then it went to Denis O'Brien, who was George Harrison's partner at HandMade. O'Brien didn't care for it at all and turned it down.

Surreptitiously, Ray gave it to George who flew to New York that night and read it on the plane. And when he arrived, he called Ray and said: 'We're making this.' And that was it.

George was an amazing guy. He was one of the most famous people alive and was genuinely so self-effacing. A genuinely sweet man. The only reason we had that little snatch of The Beatles in the film was because George gave it to us, otherwise there's no way we could afford 'While My Guitar Gently Weeps'.

And the weird thing is we were also lucky to use Jimi Hendrix,

as his estate refused to allow his music to be used in any context of drink or drugs ever again, and we were probably the reason they banned it.

Peter Hannan has said that working with you on *Withnail* was an absolute joy. What qualities as a cinematographer made him the perfect choice for the film?

Peter was fantastic, as was camera man, Bob Smith. I wanted the film to be very dark and that was his specialty. I had the most wonderful crew. I don't buy into this auteur bollocks at all. Yes, the director is the boss, on the bridge of the movie, but unless there's someone down there filling the fucking boilers with coal you're fucked and you can't make it. So I don't believe in the auteur thing at all, I believe in the 'conspiracy' theory of filmmaking. Conspire

ABOVE LEFT: Representing the trio (with George Harrison and Paul Heller) that got *Withnail* made. Ray Cooper (Head of Development, HandMade Films), producer David Wimbury and Bruce.

ABOVE RIGHT: Letter from *Withnail & I* illustrator Ralph Steadman, received after opening night, 1987.

means to whisper with, and so you surround yourself with people who you can whisper with, and they know where they're at, and you trust them to know where you're at.

It was a privilege to work with Peter Hannan and later Conrad Hall in America. I said to him one day: 'Oh my God, Connie, how come you always know where to put the camera before I've even thought about it?' And he said: 'I point it at the story.' And it's a fabulous rule for a director to learn.

You look at a variety of movies and the camera's always moving for no apparent reason. There's a close-up and it's tracking five ways, creeping in or out, or it's above the subject. In my view, cameras should be a privileged observer of the story, not a part of it. I don't want a camera starring in anything I ever do. I want the camera to watch what I'm doing and then keep its mouth shut.

You strove to create a reality of two people's lives in the hope that the audience would find their struggle as funny as you eventually did. How much did you fear that people wouldn't find humour within the bleakness?

Perpetually, yeah, of course. This guy O'Brien came up from HandMade, I think on day two, seeing the dailies that were as black as your hat, and he thought it was about as funny as cancer. He thought Uncle Monty should be a limp-wristed screecher like Kenneth Williams, and we had a terrible row. I was literally going to walk off. 'All right, you know about comedy, do you? Well you fucking direct it.' And it really was going to get shut down.

I don't like jokes. Jokes don't amuse me at all. Situation comedy is different. The greatest piece of comedic work I've ever seen in a movie is in *The Gold Rush* by Charlie Chaplin. When the fucker eats his boots and then sucks the sole's nails like they're chicken bones and twirls the laces like spaghetti. But he doesn't say to the audience: 'Look how funny this is.' He says: 'I am a man starving, eating a pair of boots', which makes it so funny. You know the scene in *Withnail* where Marwood sticks a chicken in the oven standing upright – if I had anything in my head at the time, it was Chaplin in that hut in Alaska.

How close did Michael Pickwoad come to getting the feel of your Camden flat?

Michael was brilliant, absolutely bang on, although it was slightly more luxurious than the reality. My friend Viv, who I shared the flat with, came from a much wealthier background than me – public school, lower upper-class type of stuff. So he had lots of relatives who would croak and he'd get bits and pieces of furniture. So we'd be living with a variety of quality furniture that had been left in a will.

I remember one of the criticisms of *Withnail* I saw from America where someone said: 'How come Marwood has this $5,000 brass bed? It's ridiculous.' But that's to be ignorant of what it was like in the '60s in England with junk shops everywhere that don't exist anymore. They're all antique shops now. I bought a brass bed in Ramsgate for ten shillings. I've still got it actually – just 50 pence. You could buy top-end antique stuff for nothing in those days.

Did you visualise your approach to the actual directing before shooting started?

I was looked after by my producers, by the crew, and I met everybody very early on. I said: 'I know exactly what I want, but I'm not exactly certain how to get it, so I'm relying on you guys – I'll tell you what I want, and you've got to do it.' And they did.

If you alienate your crew, you're screwed – dead in the water. Unless you're someone like Ridley Scott, who can do it with his eyes shut. I didn't know any of that stuff. I said to Peter Hannan and camera operator Bob Smith that I wanted it to be shot like I'm looking at it like the camera's an observer.

So virtually everything in *Withnail* was shot on a 50-mill lens, which is basically like our eyesight. We used 50 mill all over the film except when Uncle Monty arrives, then we used a 35 to get that more old-fashioned look, plus the old-fashioned music.

Do you think Withnail thrives on Marwood's unrequited attention?

He does in the movie. There was some peculiar book called *Vivian and I*, written as though I rushed around in my friend's wake with a notebook, but there isn't a line of Viv's in the film. Withnail's an invented character. Everyone is inspired by something or other, so he, and our relationship, and the rest of my circle inspired me to write the film, but it isn't a documentary – it's a drama.

Any memories of the pub scene with Daragh O'Malley and what you were after for the Irishman?

I do remember that Daragh was incredibly nervous on the day we were going to shoot it, and who wouldn't be? The film was a two-hander. Everyone knew everyone and it must have felt like walking into somebody else's family. Everyone was *au fait* with everyone else. And he has to come on set, and only has the one day's work. But it was a very important scene. What I wanted was an Irish Wanker, and I think he found it difficult to hit that immediately, but he did, and he's great in the film. 'I'll murder the pair of yers.' Camden Town was alive with people like that. It isn't any more. That house I lived in cost David eight grand and now would probably put you back three million.

Withnail turns in desperation to lighter fuel... Why is he on such a mission of self-destruction despite his education and culture?

Viv did drink lighter fuel, but not in the context it was in the film. We argued all the time, but never in a personal way. We could have a heated discussion about Verlaine or Jesus Christ or God. It was great for me in a sense, because I had an unpleasant childhood, no money, and consequently no education.

When I left secondary modern school, I could barely read and write, and here I was going into drama school with these guys who were predominantly older than me, and a few of them had been to university and most of them had a decent education. So someone like Vivian knew about Verlaine and Rimbaud, and could speak pretty good French, and I was just blown away by all of this kind of stuff. Stir weed into that environment and I was sort of being educated as I went along. I hate the word but I'm an autodidact – educated myself over the years by reading my arse off, which is my greatest pleasure – reading and reading, and

learning to read French. And so Viv was instrumental in turning me on to various things such as poetry, which I craved as a kid, but I didn't even know it existed till drama school.

Withnail's resentment was based deep down: 'How dare they not see that I am who I am?' In *Richard III*, Richard says: 'If I cannot prove a lover, I'm determined to prove a villain.' And Viv was the same: 'If I can't be James fucking Dean, revered and loved by the world, then I fucking hate who I am.' And I think that was where he was stuck.

The '60s are often idealised, but you paint a darker picture in *Withnail & I*. Had you had enough of the decade by the end of it?

No, we were rather hoping it was going to last. But what happened at the end of the sixties was an ugly foretaste of where we're at now. London has become a glum town, like a shopping-mall at an airport. Why? Because all the punks and poets, all the 'life' and

ABOVE: Letter from Viv to Bruce March 1987. Viv passed away 2nd of March 1995.

> **"The reason we're now living in such dispiriting times is because of the soulless myopia of the Thatcher Myth."**

above all the young, have been priced-out. They can't afford to live in it. So they migrated to the East End with its cheap streets and by definition made East London dynamic. But cool your boots, here comes Starbucks and the Estate Agents, greed following the trend. And that's what happened to the sixties: 'They're selling Hippy wigs in Woolworths, man.'

Part of the reason the sixties exploded was because after years of Conservative austerity, Labour got elected and Harold Wilson reflated the economy. He did what the Tories preach, actually put money into the people's pockets, and the young wanted to spend it on the age they were living in. London became the most exciting city in the world. And the reason we're now living in such dispiriting times is because of the soulless myopia of the Thatcher Myth.

Can anyone imagine the Germans selling Mercedes Benz, B.M.W or Porsche to the British? But its equivalence is exactly what these pricks have done. They've sold Mini and Bentley and Rolls Royce to Germany. 'Take Back Control' they said. Take back control of what? These same voices have sold practically everything this country ever had: sold our railways, sold our utilities, sold off the fucking rain we drink, which is doubtless why our rivers are full of shit. 'Shat on by Tories' has become a scandalous reality – fortunes for the few, and slogans for the proles.

It's my philosophy that money is like language: everyone should have the opportunity to use it. And, of course, some people are going to be better at talking than others. But that doesn't preclude the fact that others should also have words, and the facility to use them, and that's what I think money should be. We're always going to have a Charles Dickens, but why should the average person be on £9.50 a fucking hour? How about £15.50 an hour, or £25.50 and get the economy excited again?

It's interesting you mentioned Charles Dickens. Did he inspire you in any way when you were writing *Withnail & I*?
Dickens is my passion. It's weird, the first book I ever properly read was when I was about 14 years old. I had bad asthma and

I was off school, which by happenstance was called the Charles Dickens Secondary Modern School in Broadstairs, where Dickens wrote the greater part of *Copperfield*. Anyway, I was off for about a month, and my teacher knocked at the door and he gave my mother a parcel and said: 'I thought that Bruce might like this.' It was *Oliver Twist*.

I was up there in bed trying to breathe and this thing came into my life, and I couldn't fucking believe it. I couldn't believe that writing like this existed. London is full of statues of mass-murderers and louts, but where's the statue of Dickens?

Did you create any form of brief for David Dundas for the score?
Davie and I were at drama school together, and he was a successful musician at that time, and I gave him a free brief. He said: 'I've got some songs for the film.' So I went round there to listen to them, and it was an awful evening because there was nothing right for me at all.

'How about this then?'

'No it's not right.'

'What about this?'

'No, no no.' To the point of it actually being embarrassing.

So he said: 'Well I don't fucking know, I've done my best. This one is all I've got left.'

And he put on the *Withnail* theme, with that instrument – a calliope, and the whole atmosphere changed. It was magnificent.

And I said: 'David, you've got it, that's it. I can't do music, but that's the music in my head.'

It was the most brilliant theme, and it still is…

Did you have a favourite scene in the film with regards to its acting?
My favourite moment, which was by accident, is with Daragh O'Malley, when Richard gets that bit of pastry stuck in his tooth. I had to have a quiet set. If anyone laughed, I'd go again. Because if you're laughing here, that's not real. But I have to say I laughed my fucking head off when Richard said 'Would you like a drink?'

with that pastry stuck in his tooth.

Another moment where I nearly laughed was Richard's line: 'We'll install a fucking jukebox and liven you stiffs up a bit.' He corpses, and I kept cutting, and said: 'Richard you just mustn't laugh.' But he couldn't do it without corpsing. So I figured, well he's meant to be drunk, so we'll have to pick the one with the least corpse, and it's there in the flick.

How much did Baudelaire inspire your writing of the screenplay?
Viv used to get up in the morning in Camden and have a strong coffee with cinnamon, and a little nut of hashish melted into it, which he called the 'Baudelaire principle.' And so I used to have a Baudelaire principle with him and I didn't even think about it. And then one day, I said: What is the Baudelaire principle Viv?' And he said:

'Well you know – Baudelaire.'

And I said: 'No I've never heard of him.'

And Viv said: 'Fuck me. He's probably one of the greatest poets who ever lived, certainly the greatest French poet of that period.'

So I rushed down to the Parkway newsagent that had a small bookshop, and I ordered Penguin's *Baudelaire* and I was instantly hooked. And indeed, the first screenplay I ever wrote was called *Spleen*, which is based on the life of Baudelaire. I knew fuck all about writing a screenplay, but I wrote one about him.

One of the greatest presents I've ever had was when Johnny Depp gave me a first edition of 'Les Fleurs du Mal', and you'd have to be as wealthy and unbelievably generous as Johnny is to give a present like that. My dear friend Depp, one of the very best.

Withnail is self-absorbed, cowardly, and treacherous. How did you get the audience to sympathise so much with him?
You asked earlier about risk. That was the greatest risk, whether maybe some people would look at Withnail and think: 'Oh God

ABOVE: Uncle Monty and Bruce Robinson at Glebe Place. Photo By Murray Close.

ABOVE: 'You want working on boy.' (Michael Elphick passed away on 7th September 2002.) Photo By Murray Close.

that ne'er-do-well arsehole. Why should I be interested in an arsehole like that?' But why do we love Withnail? Well, I think young men love him because they associate with him doing the sort of stuff they've all done, or they all wish they could do.

Fifteen years ago, my wife and I were in a country pub, and there were ducks all over the place. They were very weird-looking. There were these Withnail-types sitting in the garden drinking and without thinking about anything to do with *Withnail*, I called over to one of these guys and asked: 'Do you know what those ducks are called?' And they all said in unison: 'Raymond Duck'. A great big put-down on a stupid old cunt, and they certainly didn't know that I'd written that line. It empowers you to be outrageous, which we all love to be when we're young, don't we?

How did Richard Griffiths' arrival on set at Crow Crag change the dynamics and atmosphere on set?

Richard Griffiths was an 'actor' and the boys, as I used to call them, hadn't really done much before – Paul starred in a TV show, *The Monocled Mutineer*, and Richard hadn't really done anything except one TV play. Griffiths was an old hand – it would be like having Gielgud walk in, because he was a proper stage actor with years of experience. He was also a raconteur, he couldn't help it, telling these theatrical stories. That did alter the dynamic on the set. Here we've got the raconteur, here we've got the mad Richard E. Grant playing Withnail as a druggist and a boozer, but it's well known that Richard E. Grant is a teetotaller. Paul on the other hand liked to drink, so he and I were the boozers. The dynamic switched more away from these two by definition being close, to slightly separating and the gang moving over towards the Griffiths side rather than the Richard E. side. It was noticeable but not palpable. Richard E. is antipathetic towards alcohol because his father was a very aggressive alcoholic, and killed himself with it…

I'm not drinking, but I'm extremely fond of red wine, and, touch wood as I could stand up and have a heart attack, but the fact is I've never really drunk anything other than good red wine when I could afford it. I think our bodies like it and need it, but vodka, gin, and whiskey aren't exactly good for you. I'm looking forward to getting back into it, but the problem is I'm getting too fucking old. I can't believe I gave up smoking five years ago. I was

a heavy drinker and heavy smoker. Thing is, if I had a glass of wine I'd immediately be back into two bottles a day.

It's incredible when you get to my age. I remember reading in the *Los Angeles Times* in a piece a few years ago: 'Time is the thing that stops everything happening at once.' What a brilliant thing to say, because five minutes ago, I was in Camden Town in that battered old Jaguar.

Did you give any directions to Michael Elphick for his performance of Jake?
Again, Mike, like Davie, was in my year at Central School, and Mike was a really fab actor. Mike arrived on set, and, like all alcoholics, the first thing they do is find out where it's stashed. In this case, it was in the make-up trailer. And so he got out the vodka and within five minutes of arrival he was already out of his brain. So Mike comes in, and when we shot the scene in the bar with the eels, it's the only scene we shot running the camera perpetually. I never actually cut because he was so all over the place. At the

beginning I'm saying: 'Cut, cut, we'll go again.' But he got annoyed with me; thereafter, I just let it run and got what we could.

He was a funny man and was the best actor in our year, Elphick. Central School had a lot of impact on *Withnail*. David Dundas with the music, Elphick played the poacher, and Mickey Feast, my old friend, was the guy that went to the Lake District with me – it wasn't Vivian. We went up to there to try and write a screenplay called *Private Pirates*. It never went anywhere, and out of trying to write that came *Withnail & I*. There were five direct Central School involvements from my year that had a big impact on getting that film done, because Vivian and I were there too.

Does the fencing scene still exist? Was it good?
It does. Yeah, we shot it. What I wanted was like our fencing classes at Central School, where we had these kind of beehive masks. Vivian used to smoke Gitanes, and you'd see smoke pouring out of his beehive because he'd always have a fag on in there.

So we shot the scene, and then touché – Richard fell backwards

ABOVE: Murray Close still from the deleted fencing scene at Crow Crag.

and the fake cigarette exploded with cinders across his face, so he leapt to his feet and fucked the scene up – that's why we didn't use it. But I have put it in the play (which was meant to open in December '20), as we couldn't do the bull scene in a theatre, so we reinstated the fencing scene.

What are your thoughts on Ralph Brown's performance of Danny?

Well, my only worry with it at the time (and retrospectively it's been proved to be wrong) was I thought that we might just be drifting into the arena of 'over the top.' When Ralph came into the audition, he walked in with purple nail varnish and the rest of it. When he got cast, my only concern was: 'Are we pushing our luck here?' But we clearly weren't, and he's a very, very clever actor and he swung it. I thought he did a magnificent job, considering he's only got two scenes – brilliant in both, he's very much a part of the dynamic.

Both he and Monty are meant to represent an age. The age that's gone, the age they're in, and with Marwood – the age to come.

That's what that was all about, and he was a great representation of it. I knew many like that in the late '60s. Brain-bummed, went out, never-came-back type of people. But Danny was smart. The character was based on a woman hairdresser I knew, with the daftest voice I've ever heard, and a dealer who evolved into a banker – silk suits and a Porsche.

I thought Ralph was spot on. *'If I medicined you, you'd think a brain tumour was a birthday present.'* [excellent impression by Bruce.] Danny was fucking good in the film.

His advice should be taken with just how bleak life has become after forty years of Thatcherism, incarcerated now in the grandstanding of this yellow-helmeted Karaoke Churchill telling lies. But as Danny says: 'It will pass, be seated.'

What was it like back at the hotel after filming after a long day in Cumbria?

That fun thing about making movies is being on location, because everything revolves around the bar. There were no girlfriends, no wives, nothing except for intermittent visits,

ABOVE: Ringo visits *Withnail & I* production, pictured with Paul and Bruce.

> ## " 'We're all in the gutter but some of us are looking down the drain.' That's where I'm at. "

and everyone has a laugh and gets pissed. I only have fond memories, I must say.

'If you ain't got nothing, you've got nothing to lose,' as the man says, and I didn't know if I was a film director or even a screen writer, I really didn't. All the time in that first week, it was pure vodka-driven fear, and laughter at night.

One moment Paul Heller says to me: 'Why don't you direct it?' and suddenly I'm up a hill with 80 people and a fucking bull standing there waiting for me to tell them what I want. Frightening.

Monty and Withnail increasingly gang up on Marwood at the cottage. What class issues are at play here?

Obviously, given both the characters went to Harrow School, as Withnail says: 'He went to the other place, Monty. Oh, you went to Eton.' So, we assume Withnail and Monty both went to Harrow. My friend Vivian did go to public school, and I don't know where Richard went, but he seemed effete, and had something upper class-ish about him. So yeah, they gang up on Marwood because of a class thing, which I think comes through. *Plus ça change*. The reason that I had Withnail and Uncle Monty spitting out these Latin phrases in prediction of Boris and that silly footnote, Rees-Mogg. *Tempora mutantur, et nos mutamur in illis* – and all that effete nonsense – it's all about money. If my parents had the money and the desire to send me to Eton, I'd speak Latin, but they didn't and I don't.

You reached a low point in '69, and somehow saw the funny side in it. *Withnail* emerged with melancholy and humour intertwined. Is this reflective of your personality?

I am a melancholy geezer. I tend to see the sadder side of things. It sounds kind of facetious, but I can be very funny if I'm with people I know. I adore humour – all its intricacies. That wonderful line of Oscar Wilde: 'We're all in the gutter, but some of us are looking at the stars.' I pinched that line for this comedy I've just written: 'We're all in the gutter but some of us are looking down the drain.' That's where I'm at.

How did you celebrate the end of shooting with the cast?

At the end of the film, you come up with something called an answer print, and that's it – the full stop at the end of the film. Where you've dubbed it, mixed it, and cut it – everything, it is the finished film. On the day of the answer print, my daughter was born. So how did I celebrate? I celebrated by having my divine daughter in the world, who I want to play the lead in the above-mentioned comedy.

What did Vivian think of the film?

He liked it a lot. God damn he was such a complex person. Viv hated me writing, he really didn't like it, but then he did correct the first draft when it was a book, because I can't spell. I remember his only comment was: 'Oh, this is the one.' Coming from him, this was pretty generous. And when the film was made, we went to see it together. He was talking all the time and there were people all around saying: 'Would you shut up?' I think he really thought it was a film about him, which in a weird way it was, but it wasn't really about him. It was about a time, and my time in that time, that's what it was about.

How did Ringo get a credit?

He came down on the set one day so smashed he could hardly see, because he used to like a drink, Ringo. But why did he get a credit? Fucked if I know, but when you're that famous you deserve one.

What has been your experience of *Withnail*'s reception in the US?

It's highly regarded by those who know about it, but it isn't very well known, as far as I know. Although perhaps it's better known than I think it is.

They screened it a few years ago in Los Angeles, and everyone turned up wearing polythene bags on their feet and all of that. And it was a packed *Withnail* audience, which really surprised me. So there are fans of it in America. It's that weird *British humour*, you know.

I think people in the business seem to like it. It's strange, isn't

ABOVE: 'I shall miss you, Withnail.'
'I'll miss you too.'
Photo by Murray Close.

it? Because I never see a fucking cent from the film, and it's the most successful thing I've ever done. I was contractually obliged to be paid 10% from it, but I've never seen a tuppence in royalties, which is outrageous, when you're a pensioner with a bunion.

I suppose I've done two or three things in my life that I'm creatively pleased with, and that's one of them. So I suppose that's a good enough reason to have done it.

Which character do you think of most often these days?

Well, because I know Richard (I call him fatty, actually) I suppose I think of Withnail most. And I tend to rant sometimes, and when I do I suppose I'm very like Withnail. He rants against what he perceives as victimisation by everything and everybody on earth, and I rant because I can't believe that we as a nation are so fucking humiliated and humbled by our fucking nation state that we can't see the truth. We should have laughed this fucking Brexit thing out the front door and the back door, and stuck it in the nearest dustbin. Brexit is about protecting our offshore tax havens. Period. But because of our addiction to nationalistic bullshit and getting waved at by old people on balconies, we put up with this crap, so I rave and rant about that.

We're brought up to be subservient to wealth, like the royal family, who are the cause and effect. You can't have earls, lords and baronesses without Kings and Queens. We're brought up to be subservient to them, but superior to every other nation. 'We are better than Europeans' and all that shit. Toryism has nearly destroyed this country, and at some point people will realise, but by then they'll have a different mob on the balcony, and they'll have worked out a way to blame somebody else.

In his youth, Monty 'crept the boards' and quotes Baudelaire and Tennyson. As you've got older, have you increasingly related to him?

No, not at all. My great material love in life is books – I've got thousands of them. I've always been an avid reader. I love music and art and everything like Monty, but Monty was triggered by Zeffirelli trying to bum me in Rome over 50 years ago. I have always had a predilection towards *les chose artistique*, if you like. My wife's a painter, my daughter's an actress, my son's a musician, and I'm a writer. We are artists around here. The house is full of art, music, and literature. I'm not saying that in a facetious way, it just is.

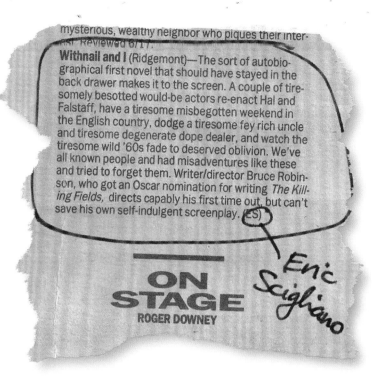

mysterious, wealthy neighbor who piques their interest. Reviewed 6/17.

Withnail and I (Ridgemont)—The sort of autobiographical first novel that should have stayed in the
back drawer makes it to the screen. A couple of tire-
somely besotted would-be actors re-enact Hal and
Falstaff, have a tiresome misbegotten weekend in
the English country, dodge a tiresome fey rich uncle
and tiresome degenerate dope dealer, and watch the
tiresome wild '60s fade to deserved oblivion. We've
all known people and had misadventures like these
and tried to forget them. Writer/director Bruce Robinson, who got an Oscar nomination for writing *The Killing Fields*, directs capably his first time out, but can't
save his own self-indulgent screenplay. (ES)

ON STAGE
ROGER DOWNEY

Eric Scigliano

How lucky were you to get *Withnail & I* written, funded, produced, and released?

Incredibly lucky in that context. I didn't set out to do anything that was going to last longer than a couple of weeks. I'm sitting in my writing room now; I've written 46 screenplays and so few of them have been done. I think I've been unlucky in my career in that so little of what I've written has actually materialised. And you know, I've written a few things that I think were at least as good as, if not better than *Withnail*, but they never got made.

So yes, I feel I'm lucky to have written *Withnail*, and living in that shit-house flat in Camden Town would have to be lucky too, and that I had my grandfather's old typewriter. It was just a coincidence and another one of the elements that helped make *Withnail*.

How close to perfect was *Withnail & I* to you upon its release?

What we finished up with was pretty much what was in my head. We realised that with the massive help from all the guilty parties, like Peter Hannan, Paul Heller, Bob Smith, Ray Cooper, George and Wimbury and everyone. Yes, pretty much we got what I wanted.

What did you make of Paul McGann's work on the film?

I thought Paul was fab. He was the anchor – the stability. Until the very end, you see nothing that he hasn't seen, until Withnail does his declamation of Shakespeare. Marwood's gone then, but there's nothing else in the whole film that Marwood isn't there to see. He is the 'I', he is the camera, and I think he fulfilled that brilliantly. Withnail had all the fireworks, and Marwood is the feed. 'What happened to your cigar commercial?' And Withnail *could have said*:

'I haven't heard anything.'

But he says:

'That's what I want to know. What happened to my cigar commercial? What happened to my agent? Bastard must have died.'

Marwood sets him up all the time to allow him to have a rant,

and when Richard does his brilliant *Hamlet* speech at the end there was nobody there to see it. Marwood's eyes have gone. No more I. No one sees it except pissed-off, soaking wet wolves.

How well do you think Richard delivered the final scene soliloquy?

I have a particular attitude towards Shakespeare. If I go to a play or a film featuring Shakespeare, and someone is 'acting' Shakespeare and not acting the character, I can't watch it. I'll stick my thumbs in my ears. So many actors *act* Shakespeare rather than the characters.

I was pleased with the way we got *Hamlet* in the end because we were acting Withnail acting *Hamlet*, so I loved it. I get letters from people who relate to that scene: 'I never thought Shakespeare would ever make me cry.' Well they are crying not only because it's the most sublime writing on earth, but also because they relate to that feeling of hopelessness in Withnail. He's failed. The only thing that made him a success was Marwood looking at him and listening to him. That's the only success he's ever had in life. And he's now failed, and he's done Shakespeare brilliantly, which is, of course, a subliminal point of the scene.

'It's a part I intend to play..'

'And you'd be marvellous,' said Uncle Monty, and he *was* marvellous. That's why I wanted him to play that scene, like – fuck, as good as Peter O'Toole or something, and no one to see it – ever – because he's fucked, it's over, he's finished…'

ABOVE: Bruce's favourite *Withnail & I* review.

RICHARD E. GRANT

WITHNAIL

Can you think of a time during rehearsals when Bruce was particularly exacting on an expression or intonation he was looking for?

Bruce was an absolute stickler for adhering to his every written word and abhors improvisation. His 'voice' is so idiosyncratic and particular that the longer I got to rehearse with him, the more familiar and attuned I became to his intonations and cynical view of the world. He fixated on rehearsing the opening kitchen scene relentlessly, saying that if this was done correctly, the rest of the script would follow suit.

Bruce's stage directions introduced Withnail in this way: '…the face is shaved and has dignity. So do the clothes. He wears a tweed overcoat. Corduroy trousers and brogues. There's class here somewhere. His name is WITHNAIL.' How did you get to know the character – what was the process?

RIGHT: Bruce and Richard on set. Photo by Sophie Robinson.

OPPOSITE: Withnail offering advice on confronting the bull. Photo by Murray Close.

The audition process took up two weeks, followed by two weeks of rehearsals at Shepperton Studios, which felt akin to theatre rehearsals, which proved invaluable, as we were familiar with each other and learnt all the dialogue before the first day of shooting. A real luxury rarely afforded in films, where more often than not there is no rehearsal time whatsoever, other than on the day of shooting.

Can you describe your feelings when Paul lit the paraffin lamp and shooting started?

Felt for the prop man Wesley Peppiat, as the wretched paraffin lamp just wouldn't light properly. Wick issues. So that delayed things, but also underlined that if Paul or I fucked up anything, there was the opportunity to re-do it. The technical issues took all the pressure off us on our first morning, which was a relief.

You were out of work for nine months when you were cast as Withnail. Did this strain add an extra dimension to your characterization?

As Withnail is permanently unemployed, the frustration and resentment I experienced being out of work for months in 1985 absolutely fed into how I felt playing the role. That feeling of failure and wondering how to get through the day was something I was painfully familiar with. As well as having no money.

What were your thoughts when you first drew up outside Crow Crag?

Perfect location, precisely fulfilling what the script described.

Withnail projected a particular nervous mania whilst applying the deep-heat. How did you foster that mentality?

My father told me that I was like an over-wound clock when I was nine years old, so playing nervous mania is something that is part and parcel of who I am.

ABOVE: Peter Hannan sets up a shot while Withnail broods. Photo by Murray Close.

OPPOSITE: Postcard to Bruce from Richard, sent after filming.

What are your strongest memories of Peter Hannan's work on the film?

Peter worked very quietly and in perfect partnership with the late, great Bob Smith, his camera operator, who between them taught me everything about how to act with a camera, as it was my first movie. They made everything feel very fluid and organic, always following and accommodating the action of a scene, rather than imposing any egocentric camera moves that might draw attention to themselves.

How did you become the Withnail that Bruce had in his head?

He laughed during my audition when I yelled 'FORK IT!' Script pages flying and my finger missiling towards his face. Casting director Mary Selway told me afterwards that it was the first time he'd laughed during anyone's audition and that this was 'a good sign'. Bruce confirmed that I'd said the words like he'd 'heard it in his head' when he wrote it.

What are your memories of Peter Kohn?

Peter was the first assistant director, married then to Amanda Pays and together they were an incredibly glamorous couple. Hearing his American voice made it feel like this was a real movie rather than working for the BBC. Calm, patient and he made sure that Bruce got everything that he wanted.

What was the most terrifying moment in the Jag?

Driving endlessly beside the Shepperton reservoir in the middle of the night with Bruce demanding take after take of the 'I feel like a pig shat in my head' line. Finally Bob Smith told him that 'enough was enough' and that the line was 'in the can'. Feeling that I couldn't deliver what Bruce was expecting was very frustrating.

What was it like shooting the country pub scene with Michael Elphick as the Poacher and Noel Johnson as the General?

Noel Johnson was utterly hilarious as the pompous drunk barman and reminded me of many of my father's friends growing up in colonial Swaziland in the 1960s. Michael Elphick was so bladdered that at one point two crew members had to hold onto his legs to keep him upright. He had his lines written just below the lens, and you can see him looking down at them and then speaking when he threatens us with a dead eel.

Paul McGann said his stand-out moment from the film was when you read the telegram and said 'well done.' (the

screen directions say 'without charity') What were your feelings as you acted that scene?

Unequivocally signalled the 'end' of our weekend, our mutual unemployment and that Marwood's 'career break' presaged impending abandonment, isolation and failure for Withnail.

How would you describe Danny's eyes when he lifted his shades after your line: 'I could take *double* anything you could?'

Panda eye-liner'd eyes, brimming with threat.

Everyone was against you – the Irishman, the poacher, the police. Did you get a feeling that it was you and Paul against the world?

As it was Bruce's first film as a writer-director, and both Paul and my first film experience, there was a sense of us against the world, wherein the status quo required a different title, more plot, women who were under the age of 70 and the odd croc, as *Crocodile Dundee* was the big summer movie hit that year.

What was Richard Griffiths like to work alongside?

Richard was one of THE great storytellers and could quote endlessly from anything and everything as he was so widely well read.

He was filming with Ian Charlson in Italy beforehand, so we never met or rehearsed prior to his arrival in Cumbria. Spent every minute possible with him during shooting and in the hotel after we wrapped as he was so generous, hilarious and entertaining. Had acted with everyone and gamely answered my endless questions about working at the RSC and in movies. We remained great friends after the film wrapped. The pathos, vulnerability, playfulness and predatory terror he infused into 'Uncle Monty' was priceless.

Do you have a favourite scene as a viewer?

When Monty reveals his made-up face to Marwood, demanding to have him 'even if it means burglary'. Paul's panic, and desperate attempts to escape Monty's clutches, is perfect. His 'explanation' as to why he can't betray Withnail feels improvised in the best sense and is testament to Paul's huge talent and skill. Monty is convinced and encourages Marwood to 'go to him'. The double-barrelled threat that Paul charges the line with when he replies – 'oh, I intend to' is matchless.

What did working with Bruce teach you about comedy?

Bruce insisted that every scene had to be played for real. Every moment of desperation or elation, based in total reality. Never 'playing' to an audience.

As Shakespeare wrote Withnail's soliloquy, did Bruce give you less direction than for his own writing?

It was the scene I dreaded most, as it's an iconic speech from arguably the greatest acting role ever written, but mercifully scheduled towards the end of the shoot, by which time I thought, well if it doesn't work, it's Withnail's fault and the reason he never got employed. As all my scenes were with other actors, it felt very exposing to be doing a soliloquy and especially one of Hamlet's most famous ones.

What was your reaction when you saw the film at the screening room in Soho?

Brutal. Offered Bruce my salary back and apologised for ruining his film. Felt I had utterly failed.

You recently cheered up fans recreating Withnail quotes during lockdown. Do you have a favourite line of yours in the film?

Uncle Monty's 'four floors up on the Charing Cross Road, and never a job at the top of them'.

What are your favourite memories of the charity showing of *Withnail* you organized for your old school Waterford?

Experiencing the extraordinary affection that the audience had for the movie. Made up somewhat for not being at the original première.

Roger Ebert's review of the film in '09 includes: 'In Withnail, he (Bruce) creates one of the iconic figures in modern films.' How would you like Withnail, (the character) to be remembered?

To be remembered.

RIGHT: 'I could take double anything you could.' Photo by Murray Close

PAUL McGANN

MARWOOD

What scenes did you act for the audition, and how much direction did Bruce give on what he was looking for?

I don't remember preparing anything for an audition – I just turned up. I didn't learn anything beforehand. I was sent to a West London address and Bruce was there with Mary Selway and Peter Kohn. My agent told me it was just a meeting.

When I got to the place, I can remember within a few minutes Bruce was making noises that it was going to be okay. I was nervous because he didn't clearly say: 'You've got the job.' He said to come in and that he wanted to look at me and that other people were going to be coming in to read for the Withnail part and would I stay?

I was sat there trying to process the situation. 'Does this mean I've got it? I don't know, I don't know.' So I did, I stayed, and not just that day but I think also some of the following morning. More Withnails came and went and I was asked to be there. So I must have assumed from what he was saying that I was *in*. But I do remember there was an hour or so where I just wasn't sure. I thought this must be how they did it in pictures, they just don't say *that*. I'd never been in a picture so it was impossible to gauge. I'd done a bit of telly and passed auditions and got things before but this felt like a different thing. We were given a script, and did scenes, and Ed Tudor-Pole was one of maybe four or five people that I read along with. We did the sink scene, and a couple of scenes from the cottage – just reading off the page. It was after that day and a bit of reading that Bruce decided that he didn't like the cut of my jib after all. So, after not being told that I'd got it, I was then told that I hadn't got it! I think it was because of what had happened during my sitting there working with these prospective Withnails. Bruce looked at what I was doing and realised he'd made a mistake.

I can remember the excitement in the room. It was in a twenties building with this huge room, in Kensington Church Street in Notting Hill. Ed came back and I thought he was astounding.

When he came back in there were a couple of execs in the room too, backers perhaps. I remember him scaring them a bit, just sort of running with it. And Richard must have also come in that day.

A Withnail would come in, and I'd read with them and once they'd gone, whoever it was, I might be party to the chat after: 'Yeah, what do you think of him?' Richard at some point was asked back, and then they got rid of me. And then there was a break for a weekend. Then I had to go back in, and *that's* when I auditioned.

How worried were you that you'd lost the part?

I was embarrassed and smarting, because Bruce and I briefly argued about it, and I wanted to know what I'd done wrong and he sort of half told me. My agent spoke to Mary Selway and managed to persuade her to get me back in on the Monday. Then I had to read with Richard.

I remember gearing myself up to be angry. I mean, angry in the sense of: 'Right, I'll show you.' It didn't last for long – within minutes, Bruce said: 'Yeah, okay.' So I was back in. What I didn't realise at the time was that somebody else had turned it down in the interim. They'd offered it to Mike Maloney but he'd turned it down. If he'd accepted you wouldn't be talking to me now, you'd be talking to Michael.

What clues did you find in the script on how you'd perform Marwood's character?

What I liked about the character even when I first read it was that I thought: 'Yeah, I can *do* that. I couldn't do the other character.' I remember Bruce asking the question, when I was first there, that he must have asked everybody: 'Which of the two boys would you like to play?' Perhaps it was a test question and in my case the answer was simple:

'That's my part – that's what I'm going to do.' I think there was something about the restraint that appealed to me, as opposed to

OPPOSITE: Paul McGann as Marwood. Photo by Murray Close.

36 **WITHNAIL & I** FROM CULT TO CLASSIC

ABOVE: Marwood listening to an anecdote about Monty's 'sensitive crimes.' Photo By Murray Close.

what Richard had to perform – the showboating, the big stuff, the fireworks and all that brilliance.

The beauty of the script was that it was all there on the page. You could work quickly and you didn't have to guess too much, it was lined up for you. In performance, that kind of restraint is a lovely thing when it's that well written.

When we got to rehearse for those few days, Bruce was at pains to say to me: 'Be under no illusion that Marwood isn't as fucking nuts as your man there, but he's quietly, restrainedly mad.' I liked that, because I thought it was his way of saying: 'Don't think Marwood's a prude.' For the most part it's the two boys. Marwood feeds him – he keeps him going and energised. There's one or two scenes where he digs him out. He's his equal.

How would you approach your performance when Withnail was picking on Marwood?

In reality, if you're saddled with somebody who's attempting to be domineering all the time, you'll find ways to keep them at arm's length. With Withnail you knew a lot of it was faux. Marwood doesn't want to take any shit from him and doesn't have to, he gives as good as he gets. There's a couple of moments in the film where you see it. There's a scene where he lets him have it, and briefly the tone completely changes, and there's the scene with the gun in the bed when he screams at him – that's the relationship. It's like Robinson would say: it has the essence of a marriage. One might appear to be dominant, but beware – don't rile too much. And of course Withnail is one of the great coward characters of cinema.

Marwood's restraint had a substance to it – you could eke it out. On the good days I did, and it was fun.

What are your memories of Peter Kohn?

> ❝ **Be under no illusion that Marwood isn't as fucking nuts as your man there, but he's quietly, restrainedly mad.** ❞

Peter was there every minute. Of course, on set he had the prominent job. If something happens to the director, the first assistant would have to shoot the movie. Peter was, and I'm sure still is, a reassuring presence. He always had a smile on his face, he seemed to be enjoying himself. I mean, it's not compulsory for a first to bawl you out like a sergeant major. A first assistant helps generate the atmosphere. Peter had something about him.

How did it feel driving that Jag?

Quietly terrifying. I'd only just passed my driving test – I think it was a condition of my doing the picture. I didn't have a licence until only weeks before, and it took me three goes to get it as well. If I hadn't passed, they'd probably have got a driver to do the sequences. There's a couple of long shots in the film where it's Bruce with a wig on. I finally passed in a Mini Metro and now I was in this 3.8-litre flying machine and I couldn't handle it. I could now, but back then I certainly couldn't. I'd hit things. Richard, quite rightly, was a bit pissed off. I banged into a skip in Chelsea by Monty's house. I can still hear his voice, he was shouting and swearing: 'I'm not letting that little so-and-so drive me around.'

How instinctively did Bruce and Peter Hannan work together?

Almost completely. I don't remember any disagreements. I think we were lucky too in that there was a camera operator, Bob Smith, alongside Peter as cinematographer, which made life a bit easier. Hannan was able to do what he did best, without also having to operate. I think that probably helped.

The experience of coming on to the set and seeing the whole mixture, with Pickwoad's design, Hannan's lighting and Bruce's directing, it was always good. Unless the grown-ups ever went behind the wall to argue, it always seemed to be completely agreeable – always lots of smiling faces.

Although, of course, during those first few days there was some soppy argument with HandMade about Peter's lighting, which under Bruce's instruction was to be made very low, so it

should look a particular way. They'd made these decisions – 'Let's make it look low-lit and shit, like it should be, let's not make any corny concessions.' Peter seemed really pleased with it.

A few years ago, Ralph Brown and I were guests at a screening of a new print of the film and Hannan had worked on the transfer. He's that conscientious. An artist. Bruce *trusted* him.

We started at the cottage on that first Monday. Bruce assembled the 40 or so crew. He addressed them and said: 'Look, I've lived this, I've written it, I know exactly what it is, but I've never directed, so help me out. If you see me messing it up – pipe up.' They were with him instantly.

ABOVE: Marwood outside Monty's 'horrible little shack'. Photo by Sophie Robinson.

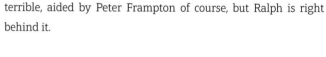

ABOVE LEFT: Marwood fearing Monty's rush. Photo by Murray Close.

ABOVE RIGHT: Sally Jones soothes Richard Griffiths having crept the boards.

we still had to contain ourselves. We tried not to laugh. He looked terrible, aided by Peter Frampton of course, but Ralph is right behind it.

Did Richard Griffiths's arrival onset at Crow Crag help to soothe any nerves?

It felt like a proper actor had arrived. It improved everything. It felt fitting that we'd talked about him and now the old uncle shows up. What was lovely was literally the warmth increased. We'd shot these scenes smashing furniture trying to light a fire – wet through. And now Monty arrives. Everything's suddenly dry. The light has changed. Everything's ten degrees warmer. He brought that with him. He would calm us down. We were green enough that we would worry about more or less everything we did. Richard Grant and me would often be left on our own with one another going:

'Do you think that was okay?'

'Yeah, I think that was alright.'

'Do you think I was alright?'

'Yeah.'

It was natural – trying to keep each other buoyed.

When Richard Griffiths arrived, he sort of took over. We knew we were safe when he got there. He was probably only there for three days. Michael Elphick shot his poacher scenes in a single day. They came and they went.

It was great to watch. If there's a better or more experienced actor than you in the room, it pays to pay attention. Look – he hits the ball back – beautifully, all you need do is stay with him – the scene's going to work. It was thrilling. Once Richard Griffiths had been there and we'd shot those scenes, Richard E. and me found our feet.

How intense was that moment for you as an actor when you lit that oil lamp?

That was the first scene that Richard E. Grant and me ever shot on a film. Okay, boys, here it is, you come in, light the lamp, look around. We'd been sprayed with water. We were just really excited. It was a good scene to kick things off with, it was gentle, it wasn't dialogue-heavy. And we were off – we were up and running.

When Danny lowered his shades, how wrecked did he look that close up?

He looked completely blasted. It's actually one of Bruce's stage directions. It's meant to register. Though we knew it was coming,

When Richard Griffiths was there, we realised that we were probably making something quite good. This is going to be good, Richard Griffiths says so, or Bob Smith would say so in his really quiet way, he'd give you a thumbs up.

When you're a young actor, it matters that people who know more than you gee you up a bit and say it's going to be all right.

Bruce Robinson, the one you *really* wanted to please, you couldn't rely on in the same way, because Bruce was Bruce. You wouldn't fish for compliments but perhaps some reassurance and anything you got in passing from Bruce was like *found money*. You knew he never did it for effect.

He could be difficult to please actually, but I can remember the feeling when he was. When *he* was pleased, or liked what you were doing, it stayed with you.

Most of the film was shot through your eyes – how often do you feel that was considered during filming?

I suppose it was literally taken as read. I guess there were moments – little bits of narration: 'Okay, boys, we're going to do the shot where you're walking across the hill and we hear Paul's voice saying this…' which we would do on the spot. The sound man would record a wild version of that bit of narration which eventually I'd do for real in Soho months later. It would be used as a reminder. They were written like diary entries, seen through the eyes of this unnamed 'I' character.

As a little postscript to this, months later, before the release, the company was deciding on the order for the front and end-credits. My agent told me there was a conversation about whose name should come first. Would it be Richard E. Grant or Paul McGann, because there was nothing in our contracts that stipulated anything?

There was a brief grammatical argument. Richard's agent said to mine: 'Well, my client's character comes first in the title: *Withnail & I*. And my agent replied: 'I think you'll find that's in the first

ABOVE: Marwood – 'a little wizard in the kitchen.' Photo by Murray Close.

> **" Things are winding down. There's a parting about to happen – these are the last knockings. I think that's what makes it so poignant. "**

ABOVE: 'Up here in all this beastly mud and oomska without Wellingtons.' Photo by Bruce Robinson.

situation then and I've not been in that same situation since. I've not known another director who absolutely knew about the dialogue, the *sound* and the tempo. It was a one-off. It saved us a world of pain later because these were discussions we had to have without the other 40 people on set. We had to have it done and out the way before we started shooting. So effectively, me and Ralph and Richard E. learnt it like a stage play. By the time we got there I knew exactly what Richard's lines sounded like, what his delivery sounded like. I knew his and he knew mine. If we'd arrived that first Monday morning for the scene with the standard lamp and then got into discussing the dialogue, it might've taken all that first day just to get through the lines.

That's one of the reasons why the film works as well as it does in performance. Because we had those four or five days of rehearsal. And Bruce was right to be that exacting. We trusted him completely and what he was getting at and never felt we were being coerced. We were just being told what to do, and actors need that sometimes.

How scary was it shooting the bull scene?
Not for me, but for the bull it was terrifying – it was shitting itself, quite literally. The poor animal was so scared, it ran through a dry-stone wall to escape us. It was disoriented – freaked out. We just got what we could in the time allotted. And they stitched a scene together.

What are your memories of Noel Johnson as the general?
Only admiring ones. It's the hardest thing to come on to a picture for a day, or even half a day. It's thankless. It's part-way through, everybody knows each other, and you're going to be right there in a pivotal scene with the lead actors. What a performance. He stole every frame. We were just trying to contain giggles because he was proper old-fashioned funny. 'A crack at the Mick.' Come on.

What do you think was the moment Marwood realised he has to let go of Withnail, because he kept getting thrown under the bus?

person.' Anyway, it's a half-joke, but my name appears first as the end credits roll and Richard's comes first in the pre-titles. It did actually exercise one or two minds at the time.

When you were rehearsing, did Bruce's demands that you constantly rehearse the lines give your performance unconscious instincts?
I don't know that he was after anything unconscious, or if he was even after naturalism. He was adamant that what he had written was akin to a musical score, in the sense that it would work in delivery if the balance and rhythm was right. I think Ralph mentioned this. In rehearsal, Bruce would let you attempt it, in the hope that you instinctively found the rhythm he was after. He might let you try it twice. But if you were plainly not going to get to what he had in his head, then he'd tell you the line. He'd say: 'No, no, I hear it more like this. Try it like this.' And ordinarily actors would bridle at being given a line reading by a director, but not in this case. Why would you? A: Bruce was an actor, and B: He absolutely understood it. I'd never been in that

I don't know that there *is* a moment. It's sadder than that. The story is about the last few weeks of their time together. It's about the end of the decade. Things are winding down. There's a parting about to happen – these are the last knockings. I think that's what makes it so poignant.

In the script, there are the incidents we see – Withnail's cowardice, his bawling out, his antics and the stuff that goes on. Those are just the latest in their lives. It's already been decided. It's decided before we meet them. This is over and Withnail knows it's over. We see the offer arrive for *Journey's End*, and we know it. If you don't see it's over, you don't know what you're watching. There's not a single reason. They're playing out the end of the relationship – it has to be this way. They also love each other, but then that's not going to save them. You know, people who love each other part every day, *every* day. They're doing it right now. This is just how things have to be. Withnail can't come with him. '*It's over man,*' as

Danny would say. It's deeply sad.

When the telegram arrives, they're still in the cottage. The uncle has left. He's left this painful letter. Marwood reads it out to Withnail who's still sitting there eating his dinner, still piss-taking, when suddenly this telegram arrives. He's got the gig. He's got *Journey's End*. And suddenly, what happens is everything physically accelerates. Next scene they're back in the car, he's still got his dinner on his lap. It's now forward motion – *whoosh*. Back to London, and Danny and Presuming Ed are there. It's running at speed to the end. Marwood takes charge from that moment. It's like: 'No – we're going.'

'What do you mean we're going?'

When it *really* matters *Marwood* takes charge. This is how it's going to be. This is inexorable. I'm leaving. Grab your dinner if you're coming. I'm out the door. That's the relationship playing out. It's very simple and believable… recognisable to anyone that's been there.

ABOVE: 'It's a stinker, Withnail.' Photo by Murray Close.

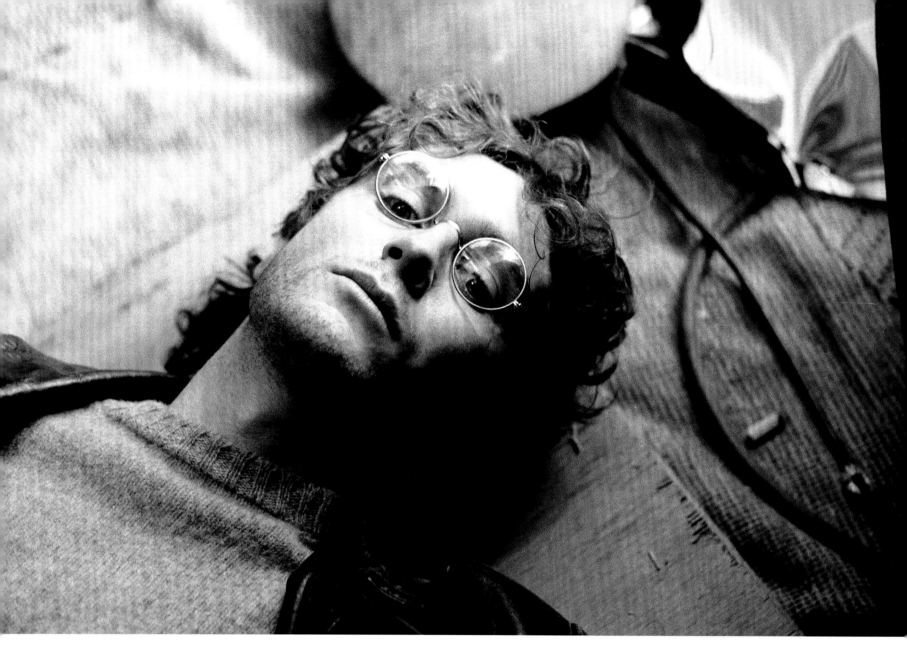

Do you have a favourite scene as a viewer?

I have a favourite moment. Richard Grant's work in the film is *fantastic*. I was three feet from him while he was doing most of it but even years later, knowing what I know now, I still can't figure out how he's done it, technically. My favourite moment – in fact I just recalled it – is when the postman you don't see arrives with the telegram. Marwood doesn't read the telegram out – we're meant to glean what it is. The way we get to find out is from Withnail's response. He's sitting there at the table and he's eating. I come over and I hand it to him, and my favourite bit in the whole film is his reaction to reading it, and the way he says: 'Well done.'

Everything I just tried to describe to you about their inevitable parting, Richard *plays* in three seconds. All the love, all the hurt, what it costs. Everything in that reaction, in that expression. To me it's genius screen-acting. He had quite a few of those moments in the picture. Some of them very funny, some quite big and bold. But he could also do it quietly. He was quite brilliant.

What did you learn most from working with Bruce?

It felt like a big deal for us – for me and for Ralph and for Richard – to work on a movie. Because it was – and remains – a step up. Technically, it's not like doing television. We'd done a bit of television. We'd been in front of cameras; on video or on the 16mm they used on TV. But when you'd get onto a movie set on 35mm, as it was in those days, you might have to modify the way you worked.

I didn't want to get embarrassed, and least of all I didn't want anybody to say: 'Look son, you can do that on telly but you can't do that here.' And it sort of happened on the second or third day we were in the cottage, and I remember I'd done something and I heard someone snigger. And somebody whispering to another: 'TV.' I felt like an idiot. Anyway, Bruce understood and he might just say: 'No, no – keep still. No, no – you don't have to do that.' Just little pointers. Directing. And we were thankful because it made us better. We learned working with Bruce to expect better.

I think Bruce encouraged us think that this is how good

things can be. How good things *should* be. Almost a minimum requirement. If you love and enjoy your work … it can be like this. If you don't relate to something or don't like it, don't do it. Funnily enough, I say that, but about two years later I remember him giving me a call. I don't think I'd worked for a while. He asked me what I was doing, and I said I was waiting for another good script, and he said: 'Listen, you're not going to get another one like that one.' I think he was concerned that if I waited too long – well, it's a brutal business, and we can get passed over, and he said: 'Look, just take the next thing that comes along.'

What do you think was the magic ingredient in *Withnail* that made it all click?
It's nothing mysterious. It's the writing. That's the reason we're still talking about it. I read something Ben Kingsley said about doing *Sexy Beast* with Ray Winstone – how he'd never worked on a picture before or since where not a single line of the script was changed when it went on to the screen. Well, that's what happened with *Withnail*. Most scripts get changed while you're doing them. Dialogue gets modified, lines get cut or swapped around. *Withnail* went onto the screen unchanged, because it was ready. That's the reason.

Everyone was against you – the Irishman, the poacher, the police. Did you get a feeling that it was you and Richard against the world when you were acting this?
There was a good feeling, actually. We sort of relied on each other anyway, particularly for the first week or two. It was more or less just us two all the way through, we were in every scene. In that first week when the grown-ups were arguing, when they were threatening to pull the plug, we felt like the children in the relationship, and I think we probably cultivated that. That it was us against the world a little bit. It worked for us.

Sometimes shoots are tricky. Richard and I had a good working relationship. We were quite protective of one another. I can still see the two of us when school was out. Not in the pub – he never came to the pub. But you know, when no one else was looking, we could

just be excited. I mean, as Paul and Richard. It was important, we were excited, and we shared it.

What do you feel gives the film its ageless quality?
I've talked to people who were actually under the impression that we'd made it at the end of the '60s and I've had to say: 'Jesus, how old do you think I am? No, no, we shot it in '86.' And it doesn't compute with some people. Stylistically, the film might have been shot in any one of three or four decades, so it's ageless in that sense.

But ageless in the sense of: why do people still like it? I think there are different reasons. Mainly I think it's because it just resonates with them. First, almost on a slapstick level. They watch it and they enjoy the comedy of it. They laugh – or they don't and they never watch it again. But if they laugh the first time, they tend to watch it a second time and then on it goes. They laugh at the antics, they laugh at the design, but then it might dawn on them – hold on, there's a bit more depth here. And *Withnail & I* is not alone in that. There are other exquisite pictures – comedies, black comedies – that bear watching over and over again. *Withnail's* one of those.

I live in a university town. And so, you know, down the years, I've got quite used to talking to students – particularly new ones who've just seen the film. I think it might be a kind of ritual. They do this, they drink that, they watch *Withnail*, and then I get stopped in the street and we talk about it. And they can relate to it. It might be something about the way they're living – it might be the flat they're in, or a relationship they have. Withnail and Marwood are out-of-work actors who aren't far off student age. 'Yeah I know

ABOVE: 'Then the fucker will rue the day!' Photo by Murray Close.

ABOVE: Paul McGann with Sally Jones and Andrea Galer.

someone like that. Yeah, we've done that, and drunk that, and our sink's like that and we've done that kind of thing.' There's the physical stuff, but then once they're past that, it becomes about the melancholy. And about how everyone's met a Withnail.

We've all been around a mad natural. You see it at the end – it's important we see him do Hamlet. He's fantastic of course. Marwood could work fifty years and *never* be that good. People recognise that. We've all known these people. You know you'll have to part from them. They can't come with you. Bruce probably lived with them. Vivian MacKerrell must've had elements of it. Perhaps Michael Feast, too – a brilliant actor, and I think it was him that originally went with Bruce to the cottage.

I remember Bruce admitting to me the first day I met him that he didn't think he'd been much of an actor. He said he'd just been good-looking. He became a bit of a star – I think he was in 15 pictures. But he said no, he'd never had that much ability. And that's important to understand too – that's what Marwood is in relation to Withnail.

Bruce would say to us in the rehearsal room before we shot it: 'Boys, there's no jokes in this. If you play that like a punch-line, I'll

punch you. You're going to ruin it. Play it like it's hurting, play it for real, *then* they'll laugh, and then afterwards, something else will happen.' And he was right. He was right about everything. It's deeply felt, and all the better for it.

What did you think when you first watched the film?
The first time we watched it, we watched it together. Horrible, I hated it. You can't really watch things you're in. There was a screening. You couldn't not go. It was in St. Martin's Lane. I think it's a gym now. There were famous people there. People you'd only seen at the Baftas were suddenly coming up and shaking your hand. That was nice. Richard Grant was sat beside me and we were pinching each other, but watching the picture was horrendous – watching it through your fingers.

That said, they loved it. People laughed through the screening. So, although we were in pain, we were thrilled as well because people liked it. It was as bitter-sweet as the film itself.

When you watch it now, do you ever feel swamped by the melancholy, or does the humour usually win through for you?
I'm glad I don't have to watch it through my fingers anymore. It's much easier watching something you did 35 years ago. It's more like a great holiday you once had and somebody took a lot of pictures. You remember things that happened and all the places you were in. You remember that day or that location. I don't watch it often, but when I do, I see more moments like I described, when Withnail says: 'Well done.' I see arcs of it that I just couldn't pay attention to before. It's all to do with Bruce's writing. I can enjoy it now – I can watch it and enjoy it, and I can *laugh* at it. Ralph still makes me howl every time he says the 'coal man' speech, even though I know what's coming. 'Cunt give him two years,' still knocks me sideways, the way he says it. Now I can enjoy it, even the bits that I'm in.

Richard Grant is very open-hearted. He's a giggler and it's also easy to make him cry. He's one of those people. I'm made of stone compared to him. When we shot that farewell scene, before he's going to do his Hamlet in Regent's Park – he cried for real, you know? There were other shots they'd had to use where he couldn't stop laughing. But conversely, there was once or twice when he couldn't not cry. I know some old acting teachers of mine who'd say: 'Come on now, get a grip. That's a loss of control.' But fuck 'em – he was completely into it. It felt sad to do and it's still sad to watch. Bless him.

What are your fondest memories of working with Bruce?
It was over too quickly. A shoot's a shoot. He must have been working 20 hours a day but we might still get to socialise briefly, on location anyway. We drank a bit together – he was drinking then – I was drinking then. There were times when we weren't just working and I might have him to myself, and I enjoyed that. He's hugely generous, and he'd find a way to inspire you even then. Next day I'd skip into work, and child-like as it sounds, that's how it was. I wanted to please this person; I wanted to get it right for him. Sounds naive, but that's how it was.

We all wanted it to work out. You tried to guard against too much optimism – it's showbiz, after all. I can remember trying to be philosophical: 'This film's probably going nowhere. It's probably the last anyone's going to hear of it. You might be doing someone else's film in ten weeks. You'll be somewhere else. Whatever – it's been great. Just try and enjoy it for what it is. And you know, if you never see these people again at least you've had the experience. You've got to be realistic.'

And, of course, one was right, because the film did kind of bomb. About a year later, I thought: 'I'm just glad I did it.' And we'd all become friends, and that was great. We'd had a ball, but we'd made a film that had done nothing. We loved it, but not enough people did, so – whatever, move on.

My fondest memories of Bruce are of him laughing, and making me laugh about everything. It was difficult not to warm to him. Don't forget, I was kind of *playing* him in that role, and I suppose I felt some kind of responsibility. It was important to me that he was pleased.

He would have been around forty then, and we were in our

twenties, and so to us he was a bit glamorous. There were a few of them around. They were '60s people and we weren't. That was definitely in the air. We were a bit impressed. Bruce was also very beautiful – doubtless still is. Most people would have a crush on him. He got you doing things because you wanted to do things for him. He's one of those people. I've met others like that, but Bruce was something else.

Just to be associated with *Withnail*, you know, whether you're Peter Frampton, or just the props guy that built the spliff, still has a touch of glamour to it. And it all goes back to Bruce Robinson.

ABOVE: Bruce and I.

RALPH BROWN
DANNY THE DEALER

Who auditioned you and how did it go?

Bruce [Robinson] and Mary Selway. I think Bruce read with me. Sometimes they hire another actor to be everyone except you but I don't remember them doing that. By then I had read the script, and loved it, and particularly loved the description of Danny in the directions, which are still there in the screenplay. Something to do with a jade streak in his hair and: 'Get down, punks. This man is before you were born.'

So I had a lot of clues in terms of how to present myself at the audition, as well as doing the usual like learning the lines – but it was the learning the lines that got me the gig I think. I thought it's going to help me if I put on some eyeliner, a bandanna, and a sort of Gypsy waistcoat and cowboy boots and stuff – but it was the lines, because in my first scene for the audition Danny's first line is: 'You're looking very beautiful today, man.' There's a comma before 'man'. It didn't matter how I said it to myself at home, it didn't sound right. I thought: I haven't cracked this you know. This writer has got something in his ear, and he's put it on paper – he knows how it goes but he's probably not going to tell me until I get cast and when I'm on set, and then he's going to fucking come up to me and whisper in my ear: 'It goes like this yer cunt – say it like this.' And that's how it was. But he wasn't like that in the audition.

So I knew I had to get it right, and had to work out how to get it, so I said that line to myself 75 times – different stresses, different pauses, and a different weight on each word until I nailed it. And it was when I said: 'You're looking very beautiful today, man.' And the man almost disappears into the air out of your mouth, because it's so embedded in the guy's personality that you don't really say man – it's really just a tiny little bit of punctuation.

I walked around Kensington Gardens for about an hour before my time looking like a wanker and reciting these lines. I went into the auditions at Kensington Church Street. We didn't

have that monotone intonation in that audition, because we developed that in rehearsals. So it was just my voice saying those lines. There wasn't that whole *spade* speech in that scene either, with the judge and the wig and stuff, because that didn't appear until the day we were shooting, because they kept cutting it, and Bruce kept pulling him back.

And in the end, they just said: 'We're cutting it, and that's the end of that discussion.' And Bruce said: 'All right.' But on the day of shooting, he came to the makeup trailer and shoved this speech (which is quite long) under my nose and said: 'We're doing this bit.' And so I had to learn it there and then, and it's in the film.

Bruce was pretty much right about everything, because it's his brainchild. He didn't necessarily know exactly what he was making, which is perfect. A lot of it comes from his subconscious, and we've all spent the next 35 years kind of working it out. But it was very pure, and it was wonderful that he got to direct it, or as I prefer to say – he conducted it. It was like a sort of an orchestra – we all turned up and knew our lines, but we needed him to shape it, to turn it into what he could see and what he could hear. He'd give you a couple of guesses, two or three takes, and if you hadn't got it by then, he'd come up and tell you how to do it. Literally he'd say the line, which is the actor's worst nightmare, a director saying: 'Okay, it goes like this.'

The line: 'Sit down, man. Take control.' He'd literally give you the notes – how he wanted it pitched, the volume – the weight of it.

What were the rehearsals like?

I went to two. I remember we laughed a lot. It was down in Teddington. They gave us quite a big room. I think Paul and Richard had been in there for days by the time I got there, and they just laughed at everything I said, they found it all terribly

funny. By then Bruce had got to me working on that voice, a little bit like the son from *Steptoe and Son* (Harry H. Corbett,) and a kind of mixture of other people. Bruce told me about the hairdresser that the voice was based on. I was like: Okay, fine, now I'm just going to do what's on the page. In my life, I had met a lot of people like Danny, which is why I could do it.

How important was getting this part to you at the time?

At the time, I'd already decided I wanted to do acting, which is to say not to be myself. (Not that I knew who that was at the time.) I was actually on the run from myself, and so acting seemed like this breath of fresh air to me. Every time I did it, I felt some level of triumph because I wasn't being me, and that was a joy. I particularly wanted to do movies. I'm still as obsessed with films as I was when I was a teenager.

I'd been to Liverpool to do the lead in *Macbeth* and had a really bad time. But that was the only time I'd really left London to do work. It's my favourite Shakespeare play – it would have

been quite stupid to turn it down. But over time, I would turn down work in order to be available for film auditions. I wanted to build up a CV of films. And I'd already done a handful by then, and it was starting to work. I was starting to 'get in the room' when the Americans came into town with a movie.

There's a small list of actors who will get to do an audition. And I just wanted to be on that list. I wasn't really bothered about being star or a celebrity or anything like that, but I just wanted to make films. So for me, this was a bull's-eye kind of audition. It was exactly the kind of size of part that I thought I would get without having to trouble the financiers with: 'Is he a big enough star?' and all of that kind of nonsense. I later found out they'd gone through the whole of Equity before they got around to me. In fact, my CV wasn't good enough to be called in ahead of all those guys who are just maybe a slightly older than me. They saw Danny Webb and Tim Spall certainly. And it turned out they only saw me because Mary had seen me on stage at the Royal Court in a play called *Deadlines*, directed by

ABOVE: 'No need to get uptight, man.' Photo by Murray Close.

WITHNAIL
What absolute twaddle.

DANNY
How many laid-back long-haired
judges d'you know?

WITHNAIL disguises glue with polish. MARWOOD gets into a shirt.

Has he just been busted?

No he hasn't. MARWOOD focuses into a mirror. Also wearing a tie.

Then why's he wearin that old suit?

WITHNAIL
Old suit? This suit was cut by
Hawkes of Saville Row. Just because the best tailoring you've
ever seen is above your fucking
appendix doesn't mean anything.

DANNY
Don't get uptight with me man.
Coz if you do, I'll have to give
you a dose of medicine. And if I
spike you, you'll know you've
been spoken to ...

WITHNAIL
You wouldn't spike me. You're
too mean. Anyway, there's nothing invented I couldn't take.

This is dangerous talk. MARWOOD is beginning to look concerned.

DANNY
If I medicined you, you'd think a
brain-tumor was a birthday present.

TAKES HIS GLASSES OFF AND

WITHNAIL
I could take double anything you could.

There is a very long pause. The Apothecary rolls a tongue over
his contaminated teeth. Somehow manages to lower an eye in his
head. He may be smiling. If Fritz Lang was alive he'd be a star.

DANNY
Very, very, foolish words man.

There's a confrontation coming. MARWOOD moves in to defuse it.

MARWOOD
He's right, Withnail. Don't be
a fool. Look at him, his mech-
anism's gone. He's taken more
drugs than you've had hot dinners.

Simon Curtis. In that play, I had played six different characters. I played a Yorkshire miner who was on strike, and I played Robert Maxwell, a journalist, and so on. So it was a good showcase for doing different accents and different types of ages of people.

I think Mary was starting to panic, because Bruce just rejected everyone that she put in front of him. Because they just weren't *him* – they weren't Danny. He didn't want somebody who could act Danny, he wanted somebody who could *be* Danny.

To Mary's credit, she was looking for someone who could *inhabit* the character, which is what Bruce had asked for. But none of the ones they'd seen had the right flavour.

Every casting director's job is to is to know who is out there. And if there's a play on with a bunch of people that they've never heard of, they really have to go and see, and the Royal Court wasn't fringe, it was mainstream, and that's how Mary saw me.

What do you love most about the script?

I think there's something mysterious within it. It's funny as fuck, obviously – it's very literary, very lucid, and very, very well written. I think it's one of the greatest screenplays ever written. But it doesn't feel forced and it doesn't feel mannered. When it does feel mannered, it just feels that comes from the character. It's completely character driven. And everything that everybody does in it feels utterly real.

Bruce and I were on the pavement having a cigarette outside Pharmacy in Notting Hill, and we were pretty plastered – Bruce said: 'Ralph – whatever 'appens, at least we've always got *Wivnail*.'

'Yeah Bruce. But tell me, what about the gay subtext in *Withnail*? It's so *there*. You can't deny it.'

He said: 'There's fucking nothing, it's all bollocks.' Totally in denial about that. But it's there, it's not even the subtext, it's the text, especially towards the end. But leading up to it, the fear and loathing of women is very in there. Right from the first scene in the cafe. Not that that's a gay thing necessarily, but it is

a clue. It runs throughout and then there's this thematic thing of: how close can male friendship be? We feel that Withnail is possibly gay, not that it's ever raised. But if somebody asked the question, you might actually go: 'Oh, well, yeah, maybe he is.' And then you feel that 'I' isn't.

Now this isn't in the film, but it kind of is in the relationship I think. That's always been my take on it, because my brother is gay, and I've spent a lot of time in the gay community in London, and I always felt that that was one of the mysterious unspoken things about the film, which gives it its power in a way as well. Stuff swirling around that people relate to which is not necessarily obvious.

How in detail would Bruce's direction become?

Microscopic. There's a moment in the coal man's speech when I'm sitting on the sofa talking about going to court and I'm smoking a joint, and he said: 'Let's do one more, and after you've said the line, just lick your finger and wet the top of the joint where it's burning too fast down one side.'

He literally painted that little dot into the screenplay, and told me how to do it.

The line: 'Does his dog get in the oven?' Bruce gave me that precise music of that line. He said it with the pitch of the line right up there. I just wouldn't have thought to do it like that – it was fucking hilarious up there. He's a natural comic, Bruce. Very funny guy.

Did you stay in touch with what was going on in Crow Crag?

I didn't really. We did the rehearsals and then they were like: 'Okay, we're off to Cumbria for a couple of weeks – see you when we get back.' The next time I saw them was Uncle Monty's house, which was all shot before the squat. I went to Chelsea and the Rolls-Royce was there. We were inside with the radishes and carrots and stuff and I met Richard. That was the next time I was in the gang. 'Cheap to those that can afford it, very expensive to those who can't.'

OPPOSITE: Excerpt from Bruce Robinson's personal copy of the script, with annotations.

What memories do you have of Eddie Tagoe's performance for his role as Presuming Ed?

I was worried that there was a bit there that wasn't working in that last scene. Because the way it was written, everyone was supposed to be getting really fucking out of it except me and Eddie. Us two were fine with the strength of the weed. The other two were not – they were just suddenly 'woo' and there was supposed to be this panic and paranoia – this slipping away from reality into some dark space, which *kind* of is there in that last scene with Eddie with his chanting and spinning the globe. But we didn't have time to do all of the things that one might do. If you looked at that scene now on the page and thought: 'Oh, I see what he wants there.'

Even though Bruce knew how it went, he didn't know how it *looked*. That's a long scene as well, that last scene. Usually in film you do five to eight minutes a day and that's pushing it.

Eddie was great. He was like a clue to Danny for me as well. Because the 'hair are your aerials' speech, which people think is funny and a bit wacky is actually Rastafari philosophy and the idea of 'bald heads' are people who don't have dreadlocks, they're not literally people who are bald. And listening to reggae I picked up on some of that stuff. But yeah, Danny was a guy who hung out with Rastas. And so he sort of adopted a lot of that philosophy himself. But that's not spelled out in the film at all, but there it is – in the way he speaks.

What approach did you take towards Marwood when he gets the fear and you have to talk him down?

I've been there so many times. I generally didn't get pranged when I was stoned, but yeah, a couple of times I wanted everything to stop and it wouldn't, so you feel yourself hurtling into the centre of the Earth, and lying down makes it worse. I've been on some really bad acid trips like at the Stonehenge Free Festival, which made me give it up by the time I was 18. Actually it was three good ones; three bad ones, and I thought: You know that's not a high enough percentage of good ones. And also it lasts 12 hours, and if it's a bad one it's just endless.

For acid, you would take orange juice – that was supposed to be the mysterious answer, but I never thought that did anything. For weed, it's pretty much what Danny says. You have to breathe. Which of course enhances the effect of the weed, but you have to literally just become calmer. I suppose the word I use now is surf it, you know, get on a surfboard and surf on top of that wave, as it's a wave which is passing through you. You need to be on a paddleboard or something, whatever visually works for you to make a forward motion on top of that rush.

'You've got a rush. It will pass. Be seated.'

What do you think of the soundtrack?

The soundtrack to me is perfect. I couldn't imagine other bits of music in it to be honest, because it's so embedded. I would particularly hold up the two Hendrix tracks, which is a miracle that they have been allowed to be on the soundtrack because Jimi Hendrix's sister is notorious for not allowing her brother's music to be used in any film that has drugs or sex. *Oh well.* They were a triumph. But, above that, the King Curtis at the beginning is an astounding opening to a film.

It sets the tone that we're going to take a bit of time in this film with some people. It's kind of magnetic – it sucks you into the movie for that first three minutes. Paul is absolutely brilliant in that sequence.

The strange one is when they're shooting the fish – it's

like organ grinder fairground music. The soundtrack never settles into one groove. There's always something else, and not necessarily what you'd imagine would be an obvious way for a 1969 soundtrack.

Any memories of Peter Hannan's work on the film?

Peter was the most experienced person out of everybody. He literally got it made every day. Consider how difficult it was to shoot that last scene – the geography of it, where people were going to sit. That would have been Peter, and then there was the job of the AD as well – to structure the day so that we get everything in the can. And then the DP and the director and so on have to make that work. Peter did some absolutely stunning work in in Cumbria. 'I'm going to be a star' springs to mind as a key shot.

He's a lovely guy, a really, really sweet man.

Bruce avoided any improvisation, but were there any moments when Danny evolved beyond the script?

I'm not sure that he was very cool with people improvising, because it would always be your taste as opposed to his, and the entire film was his taste. I was only working for three days, not counting rehearsals. Only shooting for three days, but I built an entire career on that, but he was also letting me do whatever I wanted – don't get me wrong.

I was cast in *Wayne's World 2* and I didn't even audition for that. I was flown over to LA to read the Del Preston character, and I looked at the lines my character had to say: 'This may be the reason why Keith Richards cannot be killed by conventional weapons' and it was clear that this has been written for me. I asked them, and they denied it, they were like: 'No, no, we were going to get Robbie Coltrane to play that part, but he was busy.' I thought that was fucking bullshit. Because if they'd said it had been written for me they'd have had to pay me twice as much money probably.

I actually phoned Bruce up and said: 'I've been asked to play this roadie character in a comedy, and I think I need to do Danny again. You know, I think I need to do that voice and the

OPPOSITE' 'You have done something to your brain. You have made it high.' Photo by Murray Close.

wig and tattoos and the whole attitude really. I mean, there's no drugs in it, but there's rock and roll. And there's a kind of attitude there, which they've stolen or at least asked me to inhabit.' And Bruce said: 'It's up to you, Ralphie. It's your character – you created it. It's your shout.'

I'm trying to think of an actor that played a character in a movie, and then played the *same* character in another movie, but it was a different name actually and wasn't the same person, but was the same performance.

I just couldn't think of anyone that have done that before. Maybe Peter Sellers? It felt like a kind of weird test, that I was being asked to play the role again. But Bruce was really generous. He's always insisted that we collaborated on the voice of Danny. That it was something that organically came out of us talking about it.

Do you have a favourite scene in the film?

I do, yes, and it's a childish one I'm afraid – it's the tea rooms with Miss Blennerhassett. It's absolutely perfect. It's appeals to the childish person that wants to upset the grown-ups. I

mean, I'm 63 years old and why do I want to do that still? But you don't really change as you get older, you just add time to whoever you are. That scene is fantastically funny. I think they did a lot of takes on that, and the one that's in the film is the one where Richard corpses. He starts laughing because he couldn't believe he was being allowed to be so rude toward these pensioners. I love how he points at them as he's leaving, that incredible level of detail.

How stressful was it attempting to roll a twelve-skin Camberwell carrot while acting?

Not at all. The prop man Steve Payne actually rolled the Camberwell carrot, he was a top man. And he knew what he was doing, and he had a load ready rolled, which was great, all the same size, and they were the ones that we used for the shot that was looking straight down the barrel, and I'm lighting it and inhaling it at the same time. And again, I based that shot on Rastas I'd met. You're inhaling it and it's coming out of your nose at the same time. That was the effect I was going for – pathetic white man.

DIANE MORGAN
ACTRESS, DIRECTOR, WRITER

I was about 18 years old when I discovered *Withnail & I.*
My friend Maxine (Peake) and I were desperate to get into drama school when she handed me a VHS tape and said 'Watch this –it's brilliant'. She was right. It sounds over the top but *Withnail* changed my life. I started wearing a long check coat with a tie and waistcoat. I knew ALL THE LINES. I could understudy ANY of the characters and even now, if someone says: 'It looks like its going to rain,' my brain will reply: 'The sky's beginning to bruise, night must fall and we shall be forced to camp.'

Its been years since I've watched *Withnail* but the last time I did, it reminded me of the time when Maxine and I would go to the pub just so we could order 'Two large gins, two pints of cider. Ice in the cider,' and commiserate with each other on why we weren't getting anywhere as an actor. Then Maxine went and got into RADA and I was left alone in Bolton. Like a young Northern Withnail.

Anyway, it's still my favourite film. There's just no fat on it. It's the leanest comedy I've ever seen. Not one duff scene. Every line is perfect. Bruce Robinson is a genius and Richard E. Grant made Withnail one of the greatest comic characters of all time. He made being a selfish coward impossibly cool.

I judge people on whether they like *Withnail & I.*

If you love this film, then I think we'll get on.

The rolling in the scene – I was used to it because I grew up rolling joints in Lewes in East Sussex from when I was about 13. I grew up with quite a dysfunctional family. We lived apart a lot of the time, and we got farmed out to different families who looked after me. My friend's parents would come take me and give me a spare bedroom and I would live there for a few months.

In one of those houses in Lewes, all the kids would gather in my mate Pete's bedroom with this character called Noddy Norris who had just come out of prison at ninteen. What he was doing hanging around with a load of fourteen-year-olds, I have no idea. We all rolled this joint together – it was two feet long. It was quite difficult to roll because it took more than one person to do it. But it was kind of an event as you can imagine, and we were already all stoned. But I vividly remember that day and that stupid kind of showing off thing that he was doing. And we were impressed with him and he was obviously enjoying the attention. So that was all feeding into Danny, you know, Danny's pompous behaviour when he's rolling the joint, which is actually quite common. People who enjoy weed can get pretty arsey about it as well: 'This grass grows at exactly 2,000 feet above sea level.' So this is all absolutely real. Real life. And that naming the joint and all of that stuff. It wasn't something I hadn't come across before.

Did you feel a weight of responsibility having those political lines near the film's end?

No, I didn't. I mean I've always been very political. I've always been very interested in the political world. And when one is stoned, and sitting around and passing the joint to the left, (always) and listening to reggae or whatever you're listening to, what are you going to do? You're going to pontificate, you know, once you've relaxed. You're not just going to sit there and nod along to the music – although there is plenty of that. But, actually, grass in particular wakes you up and it opens your brain up and makes you want to talk. It's not a downer it's an upper. It makes you feel excited about life – enthusiastic.

It's the best drug in the world. Hashish is slightly different in that it makes you more spaced out – relaxed. For some people, that's better, it calms them down a bit. Grass doesn't really calm you down, grass actually calms you up.

Danny would have had every variety in that doll. He's a seller, but he's also a consumer. Paul McGann says it: 'He's had more drugs than you've had hot dinners.' He's not trying to frighten Withnail – that's the truth. He's somebody that doesn't like reality, so he alters it, and there's millions of people out there like that. They're alcoholics or they're junkies or take Vicodin – you name it.

What did you think when you first saw the film at the cinema?

The first time I saw the film was in a screening room in Soho with the rest of the cast and Bruce. That remains, I believe, the only time that Richard Grant saw the film – he went out and vomited afterwards. I felt quite similar to that. I was sitting next to Richard Griffiths. I thought the first fifteen minutes of the film were absolutely terrific. And then I came on. I was speaking so slowly that I thought I'd fucked the film up. I was like: 'What are you fucking doing?' And I turned to Griffiths and I said: 'I'm speaking far too slowly.'

And he said: 'Nonsense dear boy, you're marvellous.'

I just couldn't deal with it. I enjoyed the others very much. And I thought the film was fucking hilarious. I thought they were all brilliant. I think maybe when it got to the second scene of me, I'd kind of went along with it a bit more, but I just felt like I've been punched in the face about twenty-five times.

But now I've got used to it. Griffiths was absolutely right. I was in character; I was being somebody else. I wasn't taking their energy, I was imposing Danny's on them, and that's exactly what I should have been doing, but I didn't have the confidence while watching the first screening of it in Soho to understand that.

You're just looking at your bit and see how it fits in, and it didn't appear to fit in to me which was a young person's reaction. It wasn't necessarily supposed to fit in in the way that I thought. I usually find it quite difficult to watch. The first time I played it to my wife and her sister was really difficult. And I decided to watch it at a Q&A in Bristol with Paul and regretted it as I just found it too overwhelming. I've watched it seven times and I'd say four of those have been tough.

Have you ever watched it and felt the script's despair overcome the humour?
Not really, because the humour is so absolutely inherent, but yeah it's fifty-fifty. Certainly the visuals of the film are grimy – dripping with decay and mud. And there's not many happy frames in there – not very colourful. Very, very English really. Not British – English. It's casually racist and sexist, just kind of ugly and desperate, and violent. It's tough, it's about the end of a friendship, and the end of hope – the end of the revolution. But the wit makes it palatable.

When did you first realise it was becoming a cult film?
I think when it wasn't a hit, you know. I remember the première; it was a proper film industry party. Jonathan Pryce was there who I was a huge fan of – I still am. I was really chuffed to meet him, and he was he was shaking my hands saying: 'Well done.' I'd just seen something of his on the telly and I was burbling away to him about how great I thought he was, and he said: 'Nonsense, this is your night, you enjoy it.' Which was very sweet.

I knew it was becoming cult when I was cast in *Wayne's World 2* and they'd clearly written the part for me with my Danny character in mind. No question. And they were delighted that I was doing the character like that.

What are your thoughts, looking back at Bruce as a director?
Very hard to answer that, because he's a friend. But I loved him, and would have done anything for him. I don't usually feel like that about a director, although I have worked with some amazing people, don't get me wrong. Some of them have been as inspiring as you would hope, you know, Spielberg and Ang Lee but others are not.

Bruce was the guy who had written *The Killing Fields* – and used to be an actor. But he was immediately your mate – no status. Inviting you out to his house and just chat and get drunk or whatever, and he had the same politics as me, always. And it was his baby.

I was desperate to be in *How to Get Ahead in Advertising* as well. And he wanted me to be in it, but the people who he was working with were like: 'You can't use the same actors again – people will judge you.' And I said: 'What about Truffaut and Bergman?' There're tonnes of examples of directors who had their own stable of actors.

He's the only director I've ever worked with who could give me a line reading. Because, as an actor, you're given your lines, your costume, your hair, and your makeup, and you're told where to stand – where to walk to. And people are fiddling with microphones on your shirt, putting the hair out of your eyes, and they're touching your makeup. They're asking you to speak louder because they can't hear your properly. The only thing you've got left is your performance. Everything else has already been laid out for you. And if somebody comes up to you and says: '*Does his dog get in the oven?*' Then you haven't got that either. I've always been really defensive about being given line readings by a director, because it's lazy, and it's disrespectful of what your craft is. If you don't like the way I'm saying it you should have hired somebody else, frankly. But with Bruce, I never felt that – ever. I mean, we would mention it because it was funny – so unusual for somebody to be so specific, and of course he *was* an actor. So he would know all of those things I've just said. He's been there himself. But he still stepped across that line. Because he wanted it to be like he imagined it. That's why I say he conducted it. There's something beautiful about that, that I just submitted to, and if you submit, sometimes beauty comes.

PAUL TANTER

FILM DIRECTOR

Only being able to use words to express one's love and admiration for *Withnail & I* is a bit like being handed a paintbrush and told to show your veneration for the ceiling of the Sistine Chapel. Withnail's words were his weapons, and when fired from the mouth of Richard E. Grant were like sniper fire from a combat veteran. So, any attempt at tribute will never do Bruce Robinson's defining work justice, but it deserves any and all we can offer.

Initially described as 'the ultimate cult film,' which basically means audiences either couldn't or wouldn't see it upon release, in the subsequent decades it has seeped into the very essence of British culture, oozing into public consciousness like the matter gradually engulfing Withnail and Marwood's sink. On paper, it shouldn't work: under constant threat of being shut down by the executive producer was a first-time director with two lead actors who'd never starred in a film before – one teetotal with an alcohol allergy who was playing the ultimate drunk, the other sacked then rehired at the last minute.

The story is summed up in one line also used in the trailer, 'A delightful weekend in the country'. Two actors escape London for a break, gather enough firewood to cook a chicken, get harassed by a local poacher and an amorous uncle, then return home to get high and part ways, likely to never see each other again. It's not your typical Hollywood story. They embark on a journey but are the same people at the end. Planets don't collide, cars don't crash, couples don't marry and no one dies (except a chicken). Yet it captivates so completely. The appeal and real stars of the film are character, story, dialogue and the setting – capturing the essence of the dying end of the sixties.

Bruce Robinson was honest with his crew about his lack of technical directing knowledge and they stepped up, emboldened by the quality of the script that they quoted between set-ups (and unaware of just how often those lines would go on to be iterated over the years). Though imperfectly made, *Withnail & I* is a perfect film. No other script in the history of cinema gets recited as often due to the abundance of flawless, quotable lines it contains.

Withnail & I's exquisite, hilarious dialogue, delivered so perfectly by a theatrical Richard E. Grant and a grounded Paul McGann, is what made me want to write films. I would sneak off school early in my teens to watch it over and over, and I have yet to stop watching. It is an inspiration to writers and film-makers not only to push beyond the usual story models but to break the mould and create their own. It's quite right that it eventually found a devoted audience which continues to grow, and our culture is enriched by its existence. It is, quite simply, one of the finest films available to humanity.

BELOW: 'I'm in a park and I'm practically dead.' Photo by Murray Close.

DARAGH O'MALLEY

IRISHMAN

Who was at your audition?

Mary Selway, the casting director, set up a meeting for me with Bruce Robinson.

I met Bruce, and nothing was ever set in stone regards to my approach. I think he was looking for those kind of people who would bring something to their character. I was very conscious of not making it a stock Irish Paddy character even though it was a very short scene, so it's always going to be difficult as it was only going to be the one day.

It's like somebody's asking you to walk into a pub in Camden Town on a Saturday night, giving you a dart and asking you to hit the bullseye. So I had the audition, and then thought nothing of it until I was told to report for the job on Ladbroke Grove.

Did Bruce give you much guidance for the character?

As far as I remember, no. I'd never met Paul or Richard before. They were working through things quite quickly; it was all quite frantic. I remember on the original cast sheet, the character was called 'The Irish Wanker', so I rang Bruce and I said: 'Listen, can you change it from The Irish Wanker to 'The Irishman', because my mother will be going to see it? I would have personally preferred it if he was called 'The Irish Wanker', but my mother wouldn't have.

You were terrifying in the role, but you've got a reputation for being a gentle man. How did you generate that aggression?

When I went to drama school, I lived about those kind of Irish guys who were exploited like slaves by the big Irish construction companies.

Many of them went to London having never taken a drink in their lives. I lived among them in Fulham Broadway and I just tried to think of their attitude to life. A lot of them (after getting a sufficient amount to drink) were often on the search for somebody to vent their frustrations on. That's one of the things that I latched on to and used. I remember the King's Head right next to the tube station in Fulham, and Murphy used to pay his men on a Thursday evening, and he used to pay them by cheque. The cheque had to be cashed at the pub, but when the cheque was given to the publican he'd say: 'I can't give you the cash until closing time.' So from six o'clock to 11 o'clock, the lads would be at the pub, and a lot of them became alcoholics, and became angry and dysfunctional. I tried to give him some kind of reality. I actually I regretted changing it from 'The Irish Wanker to 'The Irishman'. Bruce did wheel me in to a recording studio to re-record some of the lines. Perhaps they weren't vicious enough. I was surprised he asked me in again, but he was a terrific director.

Bruce was very thorough, even for this small role. If you're an actor in those times living in Camden Town, you're going to run into Paddies, and it colours the story and becomes part of the tapestry. Where did he find the Irish Wanker? Well the Irish Wanker was just there, and they are still there but not in the same number as they were in the 60s.

After the filming, the next time I saw Paul McGann was in Russia, because Paul was the original *Sharpe*. He only lasted five or six weeks. He injured his leg when he was playing football one Sunday afternoon with me and was replaced by Sean Bean.

How many times did you have to shoot the scene?

The scene took half a day to shoot. There were sets ups and extras getting organized, it was very frantic, very kick-bollocks-scramble.

What was it like acting opposite Richard, and did he make you laugh?

Absolutely, yeah. I thought there was a nervousness in Richard which gave the character another kind of layer. I think as an actor Richard was quite nervous, which helped the character right throughout the movie, and his performance was very special.

The screenplay excerpt reads:

More pissed than sensible WITHNAIL swivels boldly on the bar.

                WITHNAIL
          What fucker said that?

The fucker that said it has just put full weight onto his size
twelves. And they're coming across the room. Intuitively WITH-
NAIL realises this is he. A profound change in his expression.

This man is huge. Red hair. Face and neck peppered with stubble
and bright red with drink. At the end of his arms are arguably
the biggest hands in existance. Both bramble-patched with hair.

> It crossed my mind he'd do nothing in
> his best suit. But at once realised the
> futility of such a hope. This suit only
> goes on for a funeral or a fight. And in
> the state we're in, a fight will probably
> mean a funeral. I'd never seen anything
> like this. This man is bigger than Jeff
> Teal ...

As the WANKER approaches WITHNAIL attempts to disassociate himself from MARWOOD. He engages a TOOTHLESS to his left in conversation. But this one's too pissed to know what he's talking about
The technique is totally unsuccessful. WITHNAIL faces the WANKER.

                WANKER
         I called him a ponce. And now
         I'm calling you one. Ponce.

                WITHNAIL
         Would you like a drink?

No he wouldn't. He's had ten pints. That's why he's over here.
He grabs WITHNAIL's tartan scarf and renders it unto the floor.

                WANKER
         What's your name? McFuck?

A couple of days pass while WITHNAIL searches for suitable reply.

                WITHNAIL
         I have a heart condition.

The bastard is working himself into some kind of violent lather.

         I have a heart condition.
         If you hit me it's murder.

                WANKER
         I'll <u>murder</u> <u>the</u> <u>paira</u> <u>ya</u>.

His eyes alternate between them. Pork ugly. Organs of a brute.
WITHNAIL's voice comes out in a curiously high-pitched whisper.

                WITHNAIL
         My wife is having a baby.

When did you first watch the film and what did you think?

I didn't see it for years. When I did, I loved it, I thought was fantastic. I was at drama school in London in the seventies at LAMDA, and there were lots of Withnails there. I remember thinking about this not so long ago. In the year I was there, there were twenty-eight of us, eighteen guys and ten women. I think maybe only four or five us ever worked. It was tough, and of course I had no money. I lived in a dump in West Kensington, so I could identify with the film, absolutely.

Moving the light bulb and all those little things that Bruce brought to the party… he obviously lived through this as well. The fact that Bruce was an actor was key. Even directors who identify with actor people like Alan Parker couldn't have done a better job. There's only one person who could have directed *Withnail & I* and that was Bruce Robinson.

When did you first realise it had become a cult film?

It came out and disappeared, but then I kept hearing stories about it. I heard Bruce hadn't got all his fee, and that two young guys from Canada had bought the video distribution rights for buttons, and were making fortunes out of it.

I had another day on a HandMade film, which was also kick-bollocks-scramble, where me and Pierce Brosnan played two IRA men in a car with Bob Hoskins at the end of *The Long Good Friday.*, I think it was Pierce's first job. He collected me in his Morris Minor to go to the shoot. John Mackenzie was the director, and that was another HandMade film that died and then came back, and is now ranked as one of the great gangster films of the time. So HandMade had these two wonderful films and ended up skint.

And then in Los Angeles, the number of people who were aware of *Withnail* surprised me in the mid to late '90s. I thought to myself: 'Bruce's film has got legs.'

More recently, the Laemmle at Sunset Boulevard changed their big night screening of *The Rocky Horror Picture Show* to run *Withnail & I*, and everybody comes dressed as the characters. I went to a showing and it was amazing.

Was Bruce Robinson positioned behind the camera most of the time?

I think Bruce was a director who was more focused on the actors. The industry has changed so much. I don't think there was any video assists that there was with certain views, so you couldn't refer to the video. I think he was just focused on his actors.

I don't know what kind of processes Richard Grant worked up with his character. People have told me that Daniel Day-Lewis was offered the role initially; whether that's true or not, I don't know. But Richard E. Grant – that was a performance for the ages, that would have been very hard to beat.

ABOVE LEFT: Bruce performing what Richard would perfect when faced with the Irishman. With camera operator Bob Smith.

ABOVE RIGHT: Excerpt from Bruce Robinson's personal copy of the script, with annotations.

My wife is involved in psychotherapy and addiction counselling, and there's an addiction clinic she's involved with. I suggested about six months ago that they have a screening of *Withnail & I* for all the addicts, and they were completely enthralled.

She had a screening one Sunday afternoon. They all came reluctantly, but within ten minutes, they were all gripped, and then they had a discussion afterwards. So the film has a life in other kinds of areas as well. She didn't at any time tell her patients or clients that her husband was 'The Irish Wanker'.

What did you think of Ralph Brown's performance of Danny?

Ralph Brown was just sublime, and the Camberwell Carrot scene is wonderful. People forget that somebody has written this. They're not ad-libbing. Bruce was very thorough with every line, and every character added something key to the pot-pourri of madness. I liked Bruce very much., It's sad about the industry, you meet people for a day, and then quite often you never see them again. But there was that great *Withnail* night at the 'première' that Richard E. Grant put on in 2003 in Leicester Square. Richard called me and I went over, and there was a bit of a hooley afterwards.

I came across Ralph Brown one more time again. We were both in a mini-series in '99 called Cleopatra, and Ralph was Octavian, and every time I saw him I thought of the Camberwell Carrot.

Did you often get people, maybe back in the day, quoting the lines at you?

Oh, all the time. The workers on building sites that whistle at women, they'd shout at me: 'Perfumed Ponce!'

I remember *Children in Need* set it up for me to call someone up and call them a perfumed ponce for fifty quid as a money-spinner for the charity. I've had them all: 'Perfumed ponce.' 'What's your name? McFuck?' and 'I'll murder the pair of yers', and I've been in supermarkets where guys, stacking shelves say: 'Don't hurt me. My wife is having a baby.'

Is it quite enjoyable or does it get a bit annoying?

It's absolutely enjoyable each and every time because it reminds me of *Withnail & I*, and all my memories of it are happy memories, all the people involved and how it actually got made. I think there is a great story there. People identify with it when they watch it, and it's a really good movie story for me, because it was an unlikely movie for sure. I mean, George Harrison came to the rescue, and I saw on the credits once where 'Richard Starkey MBE' gets a special mention in the credits. I often wonder why he got that credit.

I remember being in a restaurant on a Sunday about ten years ago in the King's Road. Ringo Starr walked in with his wife, Barbara Bach. Ringo Fucking Starr stuck his head at my table as he was about to leave and said: 'You were in *Sharpe* and *Withnail & I*… good man.'

ABOVE LEFT: 'We get in there and get wrecked.'

ABOVE RIGHT: Peter Kohn, first assistant director, at the 'Mother Black Cap'.

OPPOSITE: 'What fucker said that?'

BERNARD CASEY
COMEDIAN

'I called him a ponce. And now I'm calling you one. PONCE.'

Wow. What is this? Really, what film is this? Where is it going? These were my first thoughts when my cousin James showed me a clip from 'the greatest movie of them all' in his Dublin bedroom just before I left with my family on a five-hour journey home to County Kerry. The entire car ride home, my brain was rattled – I *had* to see that film.

The beauty of *Withnail & I* lies in Bruce Robinson; it was his first feature film and he openly admitted he didn't know what he was doing, but trusted his gut. Every scene is so meticulously crafted and delivered with such class that it's champagne for the eyes. The characters are so deeply defined that I can imagine them when they were children. The jokes are so camouflaged and ingrained within the characters' dialogue, you forget you're watching a comedy.

Robinson created locations of such warmth and invitation, even though the concept of their existence was bleak; The Mother Black Cap, full of alcoholics at 10am, yet I wanted to be in the corner supping a pint. The Crow, even with its contrary clientele, welcomed me with its open fire. The blooming colour and poise of The Penrith Tearooms, although downgraded by 'a couple of drunks', couldn't deter me from genuinely wanting 'cake and tea'. Also, the tearooms is where we see the cheeky side of Marwood and we can understand why he and Withnail are such good friends.

Three times in one day was my record. I've watched the film hundreds of times and I find something each time. The film gives me an insight into a time I never knew with people you don't expect – two posh unemployed alcoholic actors. The unapologetic selfishness of Withnail, the solid struggle of Marwood and the utter eccentric chaos of Monty, topped with well-developed cameo characters make it a movie for life. No glitz, no glam, no blockbuster budget – it's *Withnail & I*; the greatest movie of all time.

MICHAEL WARDLE

ISAAC PARKIN

What did the audition entail and who was there – can you describe the scene?

It was in a hotel in Leeds. I can remember walking down the corridor and there were chairs sat outside the room. I was listening to someone audition for this part, and he sounded awful. I thought that it didn't sound true to me at all.

I was called in and I met Bruce and he showed me the script and he asked me to read some of the dialogue, which I did – a normal audition scenario. I thought I'd read it okay. And then I went back home, and my agent called me to say I'd got the part. I didn't realise at the time how big the film was. When I read the full script I was really taken by it.

It turned out Bruce Robinson was the best director I ever worked with – and I've worked with a great many. I don't think any of us expected the film to do so well, but looking back you can see Bruce had that vision for it.

Where was Bruce Robinson when the Crow Crag scene was being shot?

He was just behind us actually. He kept putting directions in. When we first set up to do that shot, I set off with the tractor down between these rain machines that were flooding water out and I got an absolute soaking – the two boys got soaked as well. As I got between Richard and Paul, the sun came out from behind the clouds and Bruce shouted cut as he wanted rain not sun, and they just all went off and left me sat on tractor with water filling up my Wellington (the other side was bound in polythene). I felt quite neglected at that point. [laughs]

When we did come to shoot the scene, Bruce was doing a lot of directing to Richard at the time. He was wanted Richard to sound really pained. I remember when the scene was shot, Bruce asked me to deliver some of my dialogue again on the tractor while I was actually driving away.

Bruce wanted me to look very stern, very suspicious of them,

almost to the point of being evil, as though he was going to commit a murder.

What are your memories of the bull and gate scene?

Imagine a field rising up to a hill, and a dry stone wall at the very top, and another dry stone wall coming down the field towards us. There were about 12 of us waiting to do this scene, which was going to be shot on the other side of the dry stone wall, in a paddock area. Now, we were just stood there waiting and chatting and I had that plaster cast on my leg.

Someone said: 'Oh the bull's coming.' It was being led across the other side of the wall. It was a huge bull. It raised up on its back legs and ploughed straight through the dry stone wall, and in a flash it was hurtling towards us down at the bottom. People all around me were leaping and flying over the wall, but I couldn't move because I had this damn plaster cast on, and, oh my God, all my childhood memories of what I've been told about bulls and red flags came racing through my mind. It was charging straight towards me, and I thought: 'I've had it here.' When it was around twenty-five yards away, it saw some cows over on my left and veered towards them, and suddenly was more interested in them than me. I breathed a huge sigh of relief as I genuinely thought I was a goner there. I'll never forget that. It's the most outstanding memory I have of shooting *Withnail & I* – that damned bull.

Was that plaster cast a real one?

Yes, they made an appointment for me at Leeds General Hospital to have it cast. It took a long time; in fact, it took that long I got a parking fine. They did pay it for me. Then they put some polythene over it.

What inspiration did you have yourself for playing the farmer?

Well, I had played several farmers in other productions leading

up to that. Normally you look at the script and you 'Oh, a load of rubbish again.' But that script, it just had something about it. I remember when I first got there, I was taken by one of the assistants to the tractor. That tractor must have belonged to the early-twentieth century, it was really old and decrepit. And they said: 'Right, find out how to make it work Michael.' And they left me to it. I was sat on this hill for two hours fiddling about with it, trying to figure it out. It took me about a quarter of an hour to find out how to start it. But eventually, I did manage to get control of it.

Did you get fans of the film quoting at you?

Oh yes. I'll give you one experience that I had. I visited a friend of mine I used to knock about with when I was young that I hadn't seen for a long, long time. His young daughter was there;

she would have been about fifteen. Someone asked me if I'd been in any films, so I said that the one that stood out most was *Withnail & I*. '*Withnail & I*?' the daughter says. 'Oh – and what part did *you* play?' So, I said I played the farmer with my leg bound in polythene. And she looked at me and I could see she didn't believe me – not at all. And anyway, she took herself off upstairs and her mum said: 'It's her favourite film. She's got all the dialogue and everything.'

What had happened upstairs she had seen my name on the cast list. So, she rang up all her friends who all loved *Withnail & I*. She said: 'Guess who I've got downstairs?' And they didn't believe her. So, she came down and begged me to come to Appleby the week after to meet her friends who'd said: 'Go on, show us him then.'

So, my wife and I drove to Appleby caravan park and there

ABOVE: Bruce directing the bull scene. Photo By Murray Close.

" **Bruce was the best director I've ever worked with, without a doubt. You could tell that he'd been watching you very closely.** "

ABOVE: 'Grab its ring.' Photo by Sophie Robinson.

were about fifty of them all looking at me. They all wanted autographs and we all squeezed into this caravan and I related some of things that happened on the set.

Did you get a chance to meet the cast again?

Some years ago, Richard E. Grant rang me up and asked me if I'd like to go down to a showing of *Withnail & I* at the Odeon in Leicester Square. When we got into the cinema there was a row especially reserved for the people in *Withnail & I*. I looked across to my right-hand side of the row and felt I recognised a lady but I couldn't work out who it was – it was really annoying. I thought I'd find out where I knew her from. So, I sidled my way across and halfway along I suddenly realised it was Una who played the farmer's mother, and we'd acted together in the West End. When I got to her I asked her if she remembered me. She said: 'Oh yes dear, I do. Goodness you've put weight on, haven't you?'

We were all called up on to the stage individually to be interviewed. Richard E. Grant was having an auction for props and costumes from the film. I was sat next to Tony Wise who played the policeman who shouted: 'Get in the back of the van.'

Someone had given their script to be auctioned, which went for £4,000, and Tony turned to me and said: 'I've still got mine. If I'd have known what it would go for, I'd have the damn thing here.'

Richard Griffiths was quite demonstrative once he got on stage because the video rights to the film got sold to someone else. He was annoyed that we hadn't been paid any further money. And he went on at some length about why that should not have happened – how disgraceful it was and he really took over for about a quarter of an hour talking about this. It's certainly been shown a lot of times. It would have been very nice if I'd had the odd repeat fee.

When did you first see it?

I never saw the opening of it. I remember it was coming on the television one night. My wife pointed out to me, and said: 'Michael, that *Withnail & I* is coming on.' So, we watched it, but I was not taken with it at all. I was very disappointed. In fact, it was nothing like what I'd seen in the script. But that was on television, on a small screen when I saw it. In the West End at Leicester Square, I never stopped laughing except for the last ten minutes – giggling and laughing all the way through – it was like watching a different film. And then I could see what I'd imagined the film was about. Yes, it was completely different at the cinema. It was not for me on television.

How would you describe Bruce Robinson's directing style?

Bruce was the best director I've ever worked with, without a doubt. You could tell that he'd been watching you very closely, and he knew exactly what he wanted from the script straight away.

I was gob-smacked watching him, because I could feel the difference when I came to play the scene with Richard, how different his delivery of lines was after receiving Bruce's directions on what he wanted, after that first take.

Bruce got at him a few times, and I think Bruce really gave him something that helped create a brilliant performance. Another guy that I thought was excellent was Danny the dealer, his performance was out of this world.

JAMES PONSOLDT
FILM DIRECTOR

The first time I saw *Withnail & I*, I wondered:

Is this the most British film ever made?

The second time I saw *Withnail & I*, I realized only an American would ask such a stupid question.

The 7th time I saw *Withnail & I*, I could quote almost every line in the film:

'Thirteen million Londoners have to wake up to this.'

'I'm going to pull your head off because I don't like your head.'

'I have some extremely distressing news.'

'I feel like a pig shat in my head.'

And on. And on. If you're part of the cult of *Withnail & I* – and I would argue that almost everyone who watches the film feels indoctrinated into a special, secret religion – then you cherish the film's dialogue. It is sacred text.

Between my 11th and 12th times seeing the film, after getting lost in the Lake District attempting to visit every *Withnail & I* filming location, I eventually found my way to an old red telephone box in Bampton and had a near-religious experience.

I tried to call a girlfriend, but it was a failure. Which, upon reflection, is exactly as it should have been – for I wouldn't have travelled to that phone box in the first place if it hadn't been for a film *about* failure.

(And yes, I call it a phone booth, but for this particular memory, I'm calling it a phone box.)

I drank my share of gin and beer while on my *Withnail & I* holiday – not by mistake – because of course, the film is about alcohol. It's my favourite film about the love of alcohol. The film feels buzzed, then… hung over. Of course the film is about other addictions, and loss, and *more* loss, and fleeting success.

It's hard when a friend's success eclipses your own.

Perhaps that's what always brings me back to *Withnail & I*: while it conjures the feeling of slowly sinking to your death in the mud of life while watching your friend wave to you from solid land, it *also* manages to be one of the funniest films ever made.

At some points in my life I've felt like Withnail, and at other points I, well, I remember the Withnails who are no longer in my life, and some who are no longer on this Earth, and I salute them.

God bless Bruce Robinson, and God bless Withnail & Peter Marwood.

Chin chin.

SUE LOVE

HAIRDRESSER

We filmed in Cumbria back in 1986, and twenty years later I actually moved up and lived only four miles away from Crow Crag, which was really strange. When it was being sold, I said to my husband that we really must go up there again – I wanted to see it again for the last time. So we managed to get there, and it was bit of a hike, only to find there were three guys in there up from Manchester dressed up as Monty, Withnail and Marwood.

They told me they'd go up there once a month. They were totally besotted by the place. When I told them I worked on the film, they thought I was the bees' knees, I can tell you. I still love Cumbria.

When I first read the script I thought it sounded fun, because Bruce has such a way with words. He's such a genius. I was so proud to have worked on it and I loved all the cast. There wasn't one lemon in there. I absolutely got on with everyone. Richard *was* Withnail. He doesn't drink or smoke, but he got drunk for that part. Bruce got him drunk one night, and he's certainly never done it again. He also had to smoke all the time in it, so he had these hideous herbal things. Richard was quite nervous at the start as it was his first film, but he got through those initial nerves, and the make-up artist Peter Frampton puts everyone at their ease. He's just so funny. We worked together for many years.

For Withnail's three-day session, we had his hair go lanker and lanker, and Peter gave him dark circles under his eyes. But really the success came from Richard's brilliant acting.

I got the feeling of 1969 with Withnail and Marwood's hair because I lived it, I suppose. One of the producers didn't really think a hairdresser was necessary on the film. He just thought I messed up the actors' hair, but of course it quite involved.

I had to cut Paul McGann's hair short for when he got the part, but as things were shot out of sequence we had to have a wig fitted, so he was in the trailer quite a bit. I'm very proud of that wig, because you can't really see when he wears it. I know when he does and it amazes me when I watch the film and I think: 'You did a good job there, Sue'.

I remember working at Monty's Chelsea pad. The whole thing was surreal. The art department added some vegetables around, and Monty had a radish in his button hole. Richard Griffiths was an absolutely wonderful man. A wonderful actor. He loved it all. He wanted to look as camp as possible. For his

RIGHT: Sue Love tends Withnail's aerials.

attempted seduction scene, we made it even more accentuated and Peter added some rouge and eye-shadow. We went '30s / '40s for his look [for his hair], with finger waves. We positioned it with gel and I used some clips. I'd be on set the whole time to make adjustments when needed – anything could happen.

The hair and make-up trailer was the place to be. You can have a drink, and it was always fun. You have to almost be counsellors for the cast sometimes. They might have had a bad night, so you have to be cheerful all the time and get them feeling ready for the set.

Michael Elphick would pop in quite a bit. He remembered me from another film when he first came in, and he was such a character. He was another wonderful actor, and it was so sad that he passed, too. A wicked sense of humour he had.

Working with Bruce could be slightly chaotic at times, but he was absolutely lovely – fabulous to work with. It clearly meant so much to him and that's one of the main reasons why the film's so good I think. It was his baby. When it was all done, we went to a crew showing. We all loved it, we were like one big family.

ABOVE: 'Times change. You lose, you gain.' Photo by Murray Close.

My only Angel thing?

There is one thing to be shure. In Pooley-Bridge, the nights are nightier -
black is blacker, and cold is colder (I forgot - wet is wetter) We arrived
like two exploresrs who'd practiced in Battersea park, only to be flung in
the wilds of Pooley bridge. Totally unprepared - yhere was'nt a wellington
boot between us, and with very little money. The drive took the worst part
of six hours. It rained. It snowed. It blew the buggar out of the sky who'd
been buggared anyway, and turned jet-black. Expecting the little local friendl
village pub, we found a pub at the end of ullswater compleate with wite
button-back P.V.C. and plastic flowers. Really pissed off, and foodless, we
made it down the road to a hotel in pitch dark. The power strikes had seeped
up here God knows howy and not a light could be seen. In the hotel our spiri
rose. Meat and veg. were on the move, we could smell them and we liked it!
The manager and his wife took is in, showing us to a darkened bar, where many
bearded fire-hogs and their le sows sat nattering about ford Capris and wif
swapping. One cove came in an old fashioned evening drees compleate with a
bow-tie! Feastings and I were glad of the power-strike. They were obviously
into being dressed for dinner, and as Mickey had a rent in his jacket done
up with one of sadies safty pins, and I had the heel hanging off my shoe,
they could'nt see the state of the ventures, and so wer'nt enclined to hang
us up. We ate a good meal Local moor-hen cought on the lake, some excellent
stilton, and a bill for eight quids! After that we made our way back to the
pub and into the cottage. It is approached by a formidable track. It was
fortunate it was night. Had daylight exposed the difficulties of negocaition,
we would never have got up it. It was only will power, and excitment that did
it. It is a mile from the road, through thick mud and cow stood of many creed.
Auterstone cottage sticks out like a boil on a troubled brow. The wind lashed
down on little feast and I.-We as we opened the door and shoved our-selvs in
Much laughter and high spirits. The wine addled our brains. At the end of the
living room is a very old kitchen range with a fire place. There is a beautifu
16th.C. spice cupboard, and a fine oak table. The living room is a picture
from a noddy book about cottages. We were happy. Upstairs, not so good. Really
cold bedrooms with beds you find in atticks, and nasty looking ex-army blankes
piled everywhere. We decide the bed-room is best left alone, and come down
stairs. After a while the fire is lit with very damp wood we found out the
back. And we settle down in front of it, convinced that if we stare at the
miserable glow under a log we will get warm. We dont, and elbow it, deciding
to go to bed. The back bedroom was selected as the best, and we both got in
a double bed, covering ourselves with our coats and things to keep out the
sting of the cold. My nose went dead, but did'nt loose its sence of smell. A
sheet I'd found in the box at hom had obviously had something to do with Dave
Lincons feet. The smell ahd come withus, and comment was made of them.

In the morning, I woke up with asthma, but- and got out of bed to find my
inhaler. I managed to convince Feast it was the country-side and fresh air

ANDREW BIRKIN
SCREENWRITER, DIRECTOR

How did you first meet Bruce Robinson?

I was briefly going out with his ex-girlfriend Lesley-Anne Down, who I'd met in Yugoslavia, where she was working on some picture with Kirk Douglas. Lesley would tell me about her old boyfriend who she'd left, and who was presumably back in England somewhere. And the more she talked about him, the more curious I became, until I said: 'You know what, I think he sounds more interesting than you.' Lesley was very witty – she had a nice cutting edge to her – and she said, 'You're absolutely right.' I was intrigued because she said he'd written a script about Baudelaire and at that time I was just getting into Baudelaire. She promised to get Bruce and I together, so when we got back to England, she brought him over to my place, and Bruce was a bit like 'Who the fuck is this guy who's gone off with my woman?' Not that I took her away from him at all – in fact I think there was still something going on between them! I was reading Huysmans' *Against Nature* at that point – just about my favourite novel – and Bruce said it was his too, so that was the linchpin I guess.

What did you think of *Withnail & I* when you first read it?

I was in love by page six. What I especially loved was the overall entanglement of wit and melancholy, which is so very Bruce; also the way Uncle Monty evolves from being a figure of fat fun into one of real poignancy and tragedy. There were almost no jokes *per se*, and yet sharpened wit in every line.

Bruce didn't want to direct it himself to start with and offered it to me, as I'd just made a short that had won a BAFTA and been nominated for an Oscar®. They're all over you in Tinseltown for five minutes if you get a nomination and Jeff Katzenberg at Paramount had tempted me with a three-picture deal. Sounds great, but the catch is finding a subject you're both keen on, so Bruce said, 'Why not give it to Katzenberg and see what he thinks?.' Even then I told Bruce that he should

really direct it himself – it was all there on the page. But Bruce said no, so I gave it to Jeff and told him, 'I love this thing, it's utterly brilliant.'

I went in to see him about a week later and he said he'd read it, so I asked him where we went from here. 'We already went, buddy,' said he, pointing to the waste-paper basket. 'This is not what we're looking for. Seriously pal, if we're going to be in business together, we've got to be talking the same language.' So that was the beginning and the end of my attempt to get it set up. But as I said, I didn't really mind because I felt then what I still feel now – that it didn't need another director. The only thing I'd have done with it as a director would have been to put my egotistical mark on it and thus fuck it up. It totally didn't need a second ego.

I've never directed anyone else's material except my own, but having said that, I've only done three or four pictures – and largely for that reason, because if you read somebody else's

OPPOSITE: Bruce's letter to girlfriend Lesley-Anne Down, referring to the holiday he went on by mistake with Mickey Feast.

ABOVE: 'I happen to think the cauliflower more beautiful than the rose.'

Columbia Pictures

David Puttnam
Chairman and
Chief Executive Officer

Bruce Robinson   8 February 1987

Dear Bruce,

I saw the attached in today's Variety - many, many
congratulations!

I've never been sure if the first film is the best,
the worst, or just the most difficult, but either
way you seem to have emerged in triumph. Onward
and upward!

All the very best.

                Yours as ever,

DP/vk

Enclosure

A unit of *The Coca-Cola Company*

Columbia Plaza, Burbank, California 91505/818-954-7443

ABOVE: Letter from David Puttnam to Bruce Robinson.

screenplay that's really good, then he or she should be directing it themselves, not you. And if it's bad, why would you want to direct it in the first place? So it's a Catch-22.

I was always pushing Bruce at David Puttnam. David asked me to write the Sydney Schanberg story, but I couldn't as I was writing some rubbishy thing for Paramount, so I said, 'Get Bruce.' So he did, and the result was *The Killing Fields*. I think David had read *Withnail*, and had a more positive view than Katzenberg, but no way was this going to rub two coins together at the box office. That was the general feeling – that it broke

all the rules, and that it wouldn't make a dime. Fortunately, George Harrison got hold of it, and gave it the green light with his outfit, HandMade.

I told Bruce that all he needed was a good cameraman, so I plugged Peter Hannan, who'd done the short film I'd made. I said, 'Don't get complicated. Just keep it simple. Because in your case with *Withnail*, another director can only fuck it up because he'll try to put his mark on it. Who knows, you might even fuck it up yourself if you get too smarty-pants. Keep it simple.'

Me and my partner Bee gave a little dinner party for him the night before he went off to start shooting. I opened a bottle of Haut Brion 1905 which I'd bought in a job lot from Christie's. 1905 was not a particularly good year, but Haut Brion is a fantastic first growth château and the wine was amazing. Bruce took the empty bottle along with half a dozen other of my great wine empties on which I had squandered my income at that time, not least that Margaux '53, and these became Uncle Monty's cellar.

Bruce was my closest friend in those days, and remains so to this day. He's the only person in this life who I felt was on an even vaguely similar wavelength. I would say black humour is certainly something we have in common, but comedy that has a serious undertow. He's a good deal more social than I am, I being an anti-social socialist; he's a socialist too, although he's rather more of a country squire than I am.

Do you feel in some ways the film represents Bruce's character?

Well, I wouldn't know about Uncle Monty or the farmer – perhaps the General behind the bar? Of course the film overall is Bruce through and through. There's a lot of Bruce in the character of Withnail but even more in 'I'. He's not as self-destructive. There was a night in the 1980s when I was meant to have met Bruce at some club in the King's Road called The Alibi. I was there with Bee, and we waited and waited but he never showed up. He was living down in Wimbledon at that point and was more depressed than normal. Bee started getting

> **"Just keep it simple. Because in your case with *Withnail*, another director can only fuck it up."**

very anxious that he'd taken an overdose or something. I didn't think he had, speaking as one who understood that mindset. There's something in Bruce that's a survivor. Anyway, we went around to his place and there was no reply or anything. So Bee persuaded me to call in the plods, which I did, and they came round, smashed the door down, and found him flat out on the kitchen table. He'd just had a few too many bottles and he'd passed out. In other words, he's got the survival gene, although Bruce is far more prone to depression than I am. Going back to the characters in *Withnail*, I would say those two main characters are the two sides of the coin that is Bruce.

What did you think of the dialogue in *Withnail*?

Well of course it's superb and has stood the test of time and generations. My son Anno – who was killed back in 2001 adored Bruce and could certainly quote every other line. Bruce has a marked talent for dialogue. But there's something that's very hard to get him to divulge – how long does he spend on a line of dialogue? He's more dedicated to the craft of screenplay writing than I am, by a factor of ten, I would say. If you look at the original screenplay, he's got a couple of quirks on view. First off, he'll only write on an old IBM Selectric typewriter. Secondly, and more bizarrely, all the lines have to be justified on the right. If you look at any of his screenplays that *he* typed up, in other words before they got re-typed by the studio, you'll notice that not just the descriptions but all the dialogue is in a rectangular block. He'll retype and retype and cut out and alter words to make the text comes out as a block.

I bought one of those first Olivetti word processing typewriters in the '80s that did all this justification stuff for you, but Bruce would have none of it. He wrote his novel *Thomas Penman* in the same way, endlessly rewriting a paragraph so that it came out as a block, even though he knew it would be reset once it went to the printers. But that's his way, and often as a result a line gets honed and sharpened in the process. He also does the same with dialogue, either shortening it or extending it so that it fits precisely on one line, ten lines, whatever. And

this disease, it's transmittable I must warn you, to the extent that since noticing Bruce doing this years ago, I don't like even one short word hanging over onto a new line.

If you compare the first draft of *Withnail* to the published script, it's significantly different. Not only because Withnail shoots himself at the end of the original, but also because of the blocking. This is clearly not spontaneous typing. There's been four or five pages in the typewriter to achieve that effect, and is maybe why he's spent so much on psychiatrists.

How do you think Peter Hannan's work on *Withnail* will be remembered?

Wonderfully atmospheric, and so brave in his use of light and shade. One of the producers kicked up a huge fuss about it being so under-lit – even threatened to have Peter replaced – but Bruce stuck by him. I love Peter's lighting. He took forever to light when we were making my short, but his results were always worth the wait. Peter would ask: 'So what's the next setup?' and I'd say, 'Well, it depends how long it's going to take to light. Ideally I'd like a two-shot from over here, with a small track to wind up here, but if that's going to take two hours to light, then I'll settle for a static setup here'. Peter hated me compromising, but I'd say: 'Peter, we've still got four more set-ups, but only three hours left till we wrap, and after that I've lost my actors.' I think I warned Bruce about Peter taking a long time, especially if he was doing lighting as well as operating, so Bruce brought in Bob Smith as an operator, who was brilliant.

Going back to the strength of that screenplay, Bruce didn't really need any miracle workers either on the floor or in the cutting room. It was *there* on the page – all you had to do, whoever you were, whether you were the cameraman, the editor, composer, or even the director – was just deliver what the man's written on the page, and you won't go wrong in terms of his vision. You may go wrong with respect to the box office, but in terms of translating this man's vision onto the silver screen, don't change a thing. That's why I didn't want to direct it because – what's the point? I'm going to fuck with it, and

ABOVE: Dearest friends, Bruce and Andrew Birkin pretending to be Hunter S. Thompson. Photo By Bee Gilbert.

effectively implant my own ego on it, and it didn't need anybody else's ego. It just needed Bruce.

I think that's why it translated so well, that nobody stepped out of line except that one producer, Denis O'Brien. He thought the picture should be more like a *Carry On*. The great thing about *Withnail* is that it's not written as a comedy. It's a slice of life. It's true to its origins, and the origin is Bruce. I can't think of anything in there that was written for laughs.

What do you think of the original pieces on the soundtrack?
I think they're great. I thought Dundas' score perfectly balanced the Hendrix. It gave it a certain sweetness, perhaps for me a little too sweet at times. Again, though, it wasn't the composer pushing his own ego. The great Russian director Andrei Tarkovsky said that, in principle, no movie should need music, but in practice, he'd never managed to make a movie that didn't need music.

In my view, music works best in a movie not when it's underlining what the script or the director or the actors have failed to transmit emotionally, but as a counterpoint to what's taking place on the screen. For instance, many years ago for the TV version of *Brideshead Revisited*, Geoffrey Burgon was given a

free hand with the music. There was a sequence where Sebastian and Charles are getting arseholed up at the castle in the wine cellar, pulling out the bottles and getting drunk, and dancing around a fountain outside in the moonlight. Many a composer would either have not scored any music to it or else used what I call jaunty music to underline the fact that 'we're all having a good time here, folks.' Instead of which Burgon introduces a very melancholic theme, and it's beautiful because if you watch that scene without music – okay, they're getting a bit pissed, but we assume that it's a fun sequence – but by adding this rather baleful piece of music, you get a different counterpoint and suddenly this is not what it seems, and drops the hint that Sebastian will wind up an alcoholic. In *Withnail*, what David Dundas did so well was to counterpoint what was happening on screen, rather than simply underlining what was already pretty obvious.

Where did you first see the film and what did you think of it?
I was in America when it first came out, but when I did see it of course I loved it. So often when you read a script, the finished film is a big disappointment, not least because you've visualised it in your mind, and what the director delivers is less than the sum of

its parts, however good those parts might be. Not so with *Withnail*: the film is far greater than the sum of its parts.

I talked to Bruce quite a few times while they were shooting, and I remember one time he was in despair over a scene in the park where Richard [E. Grant] has to say: 'I'm in a park and I'm practically dead.' Bruce wanted the emphasis on the 'park' but Richard kept putting the stress on 'dead', which misses the humour. Bruce felt that he couldn't get through how he wanted it said without line-directing it himself. As we know, most actors are not keen on being line-directed; Richard Griffiths initially resented it, but then realised that sometimes you have to get line-direction, especially if the director had written it himself. If someone else has written the screenplay, then okay, the actor is entitled to put his own interpretation on the line. But if *you've* written it, you know what was running through your mind when you wrote it, and therefore, without claiming to be an actor yourself, you can lay the emphasis where it should be. Of course, occasionally an actor's reading works better than what you had in mind, which is why it's always worth hearing their interpretation first, but if it isn't, and you wrote it, why not offer them the way you heard it in your head?

I think Bruce pretty much made his actors stick to the dialogue that he'd written and I don't think there was much ad-libbing. You couldn't really improve on that dialogue. I gave Bruce one line, and it wasn't even my line: it was J.M. Barrie's. I found it in one of Barrie's notebooks: 'Even a stopped clock gets it right twice a day, but I never got it right in my whole life,' or some such line. I take credit for absolutely nothing in the movie, except Bruce claimed the original of Withnail's kitchen sink was the sink in my basement place during the '70s. It was pretty disgusting. David Puttnam's wife used to come around once a week and cleaned it up as I was so absorbed in what I was writing, I didn't even notice. I was just living on cigarettes and coffee and to hell with the rest of life.

Did you have a favourite scene?

In that film *When Harry Met Sally*, when the girl's faking an orgasm – that's the moment everyone remembers. What the rest of the film is about, God only knows – I've long forgotten it. But the thing about *Withnail* is that you can't dissect it. The entire movie is the moment.

You voted for *Withnail & I* in the BSI director's poll. What do you think the film will be best remembered for?

Well, I don't think it needs to be remembered – it's an ongoing experience. I think it's fresh to each generation – viz. my daughter Emily – she's twelve and it's one of her favourite movies. We all know that humour dates quicker than anything. I mean, look at Shakespeare's so-called 'comedies'. From a dialogue point of view all those puns seem so heavy-handed, although they had the Elizabethans rolling in the aisles. The tragedies have certainly survived, but the comedies not so much. Comedy goes off quicker than fish. Even Buster Keaton's pictures seem kind of laboured when you look at them now. *Withnail* I saw over the shoulder of my daughter about a year ago, and it hasn't dated at all. And I think the reason is that it's an utterly honest movie, and so true to Bruce, who hasn't dated either, other than being a bit wrinkled round the edges. It's true to those two sides of his character. Nothing is in there to gain an extra few quid at the box office. It's a piece of life, a slice of Bruce's life. So I don't think that it's a film that needs to be remembered as it will always be current, with a life expectancy of many decades to come. 'What a piece of work is a man.' I know it's Shakespeare, but as an ending it couldn't be bettered, and as fitting and timely as Withnail himself. The whole movie is such a miraculous balance between laughter and inward tears, and after all that's life. Life is laughter and inward tears.

ABOVE: 'That's right. Put on the gloves. Don't attempt anything without the gloves.'

THE SCREENPLAY

BY MARTIN KEADY

One of the many reasons why *Withnail & I* is such a great screenplay is that it had such a long gestation or creation period. As Bruce Robinson wrote in the 10th anniversary edition of the screenplay: 'Viv and I lived *Withnail & I* for a long time before that weird thing happened in my head, and I had to sit at the kitchen table and try and write it down'. From Robinson first meeting Viv MacKerrell, the inspiration for Withnail, in 1964 to the film's release in 1987, nearly a quarter of a century passed. It is perhaps the definitive example of why a screenplay must be continually written and rewritten, first in the imagination and then on paper or a computer screen, until it is as good as it can possibly be. And as a screenplay, *Withnail & I* really is as good as it gets.

In addition, the undeniable literary quality of the screenplay of *Withnail & I*, which also sets it apart from most other screenplays, is surely partly because Bruce Robinson originally wrote the story as a novel. He did so in the period in which the film is set: the last few months of what Danny the Dealer calls 'the greatest decade in the history of mankind'. However, it would be another two decades before *Withnail & I* became a screenplay.

After emerging from the epic squalor in which he had lived for nearly a decade after leaving drama school and appearing in Franco Zeffirelli's 1968 film of *Romeo and Juliet*, Robinson committed himself to writing at the end of the 1970s, mainly because acting work had dried up. First, an English film producer, Mody Schreiber, read the original novel and paid him to adapt it into a screenplay. Then, Robinson got perhaps the biggest break that any unknown screenwriter has ever had when David Puttnam hired him to write the screenplay for *The Killing Fields*. The film was an enormous box-office and critical success, and Robinson became one of the few first-time screenwriters to be nominated for an Oscar®. Even more

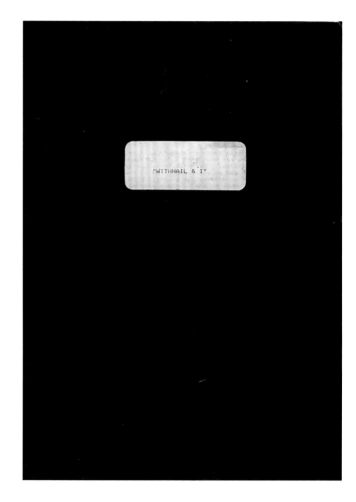

importantly, it meant he was able to make his screenplay for *Withnail & I* into a film.

Unlike *The Killing Fields*, the script for *Withnail & I* was not Oscar®-nominated; in fact, the only award it won upon the film's release was the considerably less prestigious Best Screenplay Award at the 1988 *Evening Standard* British Film Awards. Over time, however, it has eclipsed the instant success of *The Killing Fields* script, to the extent that it is now generally regarded as one of the greatest screenplays ever written.

THIS SPREAD: Bruce Robinson's personal copy of the script.

25

Revised 14/6/86. FINAL

WITNAIL & I

by

~~BRUCE ROBINSON~~

HAROLD SPIT

Royal ct
730-1745

(c)   HandMade Films (Productions) Ltd
26, Cadogan Square.
LONDON. SW1XOJP.

```
                    MARWOOD
                 Calm down. Calm down.

The person offering this advice isn't entirely calm himself. Ex-
pecting the dreadful MARWOOD attempts to get closer to the door.

                    WITHNAIL
              How dare you call me inhumane.

                    MARWOOD
              I didn't call you inhumane. You
              merely imagined that. Calm down.

                    WITHNAIL
              Right you fucker. I'm gonna do
              the washing up.

The crisis has focused. MARWOOD moves in to prevent a development.

                    MARWOOD
              You can't. It's impossible. I
              swear to you. I've looked into it.

A cross between a scuffle and a waltz. MARWOOD leading in both.
```

ABOVE: Excerpt from Bruce Robinson's personal copy of the script.

The Plot

On a first reading, the plot of *Withnail & I* appears negligible, if not non-existent. It was memorably condensed down by one reviewer to just three words, '*Here. There. Here*,' aping Jake the Poacher to summarise the journey from Camden Town to Cumbria, and back again, that is ostensibly the plot.

Of course, *Withnail & I* is really about ambition and its death: *Hamlet*, and specifically an actor's desire to play its title role, is the key to the story. Almost at the outset, Monty, a former 'thesbian' himself, proclaims: 'It is the most shattering experience of a young man's life, when one morning he awakes, and quite reasonably says to himself, I will *never* play the Dane. When that moment comes, one's ambition ceases…' Ultimately, that fate befalls Withnail himself after Marwood leaves, when he briefly stops playing himself (the role he was born for) to perform a *Hamlet* soliloquy brilliantly, if only for an audience of rain-drenched wolves.

Withnail & I is also a 'Buddy Movie', a film in which an apparently mismatched pair of characters have to work together for their mutual benefit, the original and best example of which is Laurel and Hardy. But there is also the 'Bad Buddy Movie', or story, in which a mismatched pairing do not work together but gradually work themselves apart.

Withnail is an appalling friend to Marwood, behaving abominably towards him throughout. Clearly, Withnail is the flatmate from hell, ignoring household chores and reacting furiously when this is pointed out to him. He then effectively proceeds to act as Marwood's pimp, securing access to Monty's cottage by telling his uncle that Marwood is a tart. He also abandons Marwood to a bull, suggests that Marwood 'offer' himself to Poacher Jake when he thinks the cottage is being broken into, and drives Marwood back to London while utterly inebriated.

So why does Marwood put up with Withnail at all? Perhaps Bruce Robinson himself explained why when he wrote about Vivian MacKerrell: 'Everyone loved Viv. He wasn't a bad actor (although when we left Central School he hardly ever got a job).

Wasn't a bad writer either (although I don't ever remember him writing anything). The reality is that, if he had acted, or had written, he wouldn't have excelled at either because the interest wasn't there. What Vivian was brilliant at was being Vivian. That was his genius, and everyone who ever met him was overwhelmed by it.' The same is true of Withnail, who is also utterly himself. Despite behaving dreadfully, he usually does so with such charm and brio that even apparently unforgivable actions somehow become forgiveable.

The 'Bad Buddy' story exists throughout almost all storytelling. It is certainly there in Shakespeare, especially in the form of Falstaff and Hal, who Withnail and Marwood are often compared to. It is also there in *The Great Gatsby*, in which the millionaire bootlegger Gatsby enlists the help of his relatively penniless neighbour, Nick Carraway, effectively to act as his 'pimp' (which, ironically, both Withnail and Monty regard as the quintessential insult, even though both of them often act like one), by arranging the initial clandestine meeting with his long-lost love, Daisy.

In fact, the Untrustworthy Friend is so ubiquitous in storytelling that it suggests a universal truth: that almost everyone (in particular, almost every man) has had a friend like Withnail, or Vivian MacKerrell, or Falstaff, who introduces them to a world they had not known before (usually one associated with excess and even criminality), which to begin with is irresistible but eventually, like the friend themselves, has to be left behind.

Consequently, during the story, the twin poles of the relationship can be exchanged. Put simply, the apparently 'good' buddy (Hal, Nick Carraway and Marwood) possibly proves capable of behaviour as bad or perhaps even a little worse than that of the supposed 'bad' buddy (Falstaff, Gatsby and Withnail). Indeed, perhaps it is only by behaving in a worse, or at least more ruthless, manner than their former friend that they can rid themselves of them. Hal shows all the ruthlessness of a king by rejecting Falstaff when he makes a competing claim for his loyalty; Nick Carraway, in arranging that first meeting with Daisy, unwittingly sets Gatsby on the path to his destruction; and, finally, there is Marwood's succinct but still brutal rejection of Withnail.

It is not one of the most famous lines in *Withnail & I*, but it is nevertheless vital. Marwood, having failed to dissuade Withnail from accompanying him to the station, finally tells him, 'I really don't want you to'. It is clear, without being said, that there is no possibility of their meeting again, in Manchester or anywhere else. Withnail may have behaved appallingly to Marwood throughout the story, but ultimately it is Marwood who ends the relationship, presumably believing that he must rid himself of Withnail if he is ever to fully develop, both as a person and as an actor. Consequently, he judges that this most fantastical of friendships has finally run its course.

The Dialogue

With what are perhaps the two finest (or at the very least two of the most quoted) screenplays ever written – *Withnail & I* and *Casablanca* – it is possible to open either script at random and alight on a great line, one that is both memorable (and therefore quotable) *and* appropriate to that moment in the story. In an unscientific experiment I once conducted (one with all the academic rigour of Danny's 'Bottle of Piss' experiment or invention), the line I chanced upon was, 'We've gone on holiday by mistake'. Not only is it one of the many lines from the script that have now entered the lexicon (particularly that of film lovers), but it perfectly captures Withnail's utterly non-committal approach to life, namely that he will never take responsibility for his actions, even for one so mundane as deciding to take a trip.

Of course, the three main characters in *Withnail & I* are all actors, or, in Monty's case, former actors. Consequently, it is perhaps unsurprising that the script's dialogue should be so marvellous and so memorable, because, as actors, Withnail, Marwood and Monty have spent their life memorising and reciting great lines from plays or poems. Indeed, there is a selection of *actual* quotations and allusions in the script, made up of writers as diverse as H.E. Bates and Baudelaire.

In a way, that is Shakespearian, as Shakespeare himself shamelessly stole from almost every major Classical and Renaissance author, from Ovid to Spencer, especially as there

                    MARWOOD
        What happened to your cigar commercial?

                    WITHNAIL
        That's what I wanna know. What
        happened to my cigar commercial?
        What's happened to my agent? The
        bastard must have died.

                    MARWOOD
        September. It's a bad patch.

                    WITHNAIL
        Rubbish. I haven't seen Gielgud
        down the Labour Exchange.

WITHNAIL is beginning to look like some minor character from
a 19th century Russian novel. Withnailavich. Incidental to
the plot.

        Why doesn't he retire ...
            (Grabs newspaper)
        Look at this little bastard. "Boy
        lands plum role for top Italian
        director." Course he does. Prob-
        ably on a tenner a day. And I know
        what for. Two pound ten a tit and
        a fiver for his arse...

MARWOOD has had enough of it. Stubs his cigarette and walks
away. WITHNAIL is becoming unusual. He follows into the kitchen. Looks with disgust at MARWOOD who's got a fork going in
a honey pot. Muttering invective about the temperature he
poles off for his clothes. A thought suddenly occurs and he
turns accusingly.

                    WITHNAIL
        Have you been at the controls?

                    MARWOOD
        What are you talking about?

                    WITHNAIL
        The thermostats. What have you
        done to them?

                    MARWOOD
        Haven't touched them.

                    WITHNAIL
        Then why has my head gone numb?

Some sort of climax approaches.

        I must have some booze. I
        demand to have some booze.

His eyes sweep the room. Hone in on a can of Ronsonal

                    MARWOOD
        I wouldn't drink that if I was you.

                    WITHNAIL
        Why not? Why not?

                    MARWOOD
        Because I don't advise it. Even Wankers
        on the site wouldn't drink that. That's
        worse than meths.

                    WITHNAIL
        Nonsense. This is a far superior drink
        to meths. The Wankers don't drink it
        because they can't afford it.

Levering the cap with his teeth he tears it off. The mouth
opens with a bilious cackle and throwing his head back
WITHNAIL downs the petrol in one. A falsetto whine follows
as he comes up fighting for air. MARWOOD looks worried...

        Have we got any more?

MARWOOD looks more worried. Shakes his head and steps back.
This drug-crazed fool in overcoat and underpants seems
poised to kill.

        Liar. What's in your tool box?

                    MARWOOD
        We have nothing. Sit down.

                    WITHNAIL
        Liar. You've got anti-freeze.

One comes on and one backs off. The latter with certain
urgency.
                    MARWOOD
        You bloody fool. You should
        never mix your drinks!

The joke is an accident. It stops WITHNAIL in his tracks.
This is evidently the funniest thing he's ever heard.
Barking with hysteria he staggers forward. Suddenly he's
down. He throws up on MARWOOD's shoes. However. We'll be
spared visuals of this incident.

Mercifully all we'll see is his reaction. The Victim may
mutter "Oh, God, no." And on the other hand he may not.
Some MUSIC gets in here. A single bleak electric guitar.

INT. KITCHEN. APARTMENT. DAY.   12

The MUSIC will continue until I tell it to stop. MARWOOD
has his boots on the kitchen table. He's scrubbed them and
applies perfume. The door bell rings and he freezes. As he
moves he knocks the essence of petunia all over his
trousers. No time to swear coz he's heading for the living
room. WITHNAIL is stretched along the couch under his
overcoat. He squints up with equal alarm.

THIS SPREAD: Excerpts from Bruce Robinson's personal copy of the script, with annotations.

was no concept of copyright, let alone a copyright law, when he wrote. However, what is truly Shakespearean about the screenplay for *Withnail & I* is that its 'best' quotations are not actually quotations at all, but self-inventions. Again turning at random to different pages in the script, two of the finest examples are: 'My heart's beating like a fucked clock', the greatest description ever of the anxiety induced by fear of an overdose; and '*Free* to those that can afford it, *very expensive* to those that can't', which is a near-perfect distillation of the sheer iniquity of the British class system.

One of the most enduring early reviews of *Withnail & I* was by Dave Kehr of the *Chicago Tribune*, who said of its ending: 'Marwood, the film implies, will leave this life behind and go on to great things, while Withnail will be mired in it forever, a forgotten Falstaff to Marwood's striding Prince Hal. Self-dramatization is one thing; self-Shakespearization is something

else.' In fact, writing *Withnail & I* was Bruce Robinson's own act of 'self-Shakespearization', willing himself (pun intended) to write something as eternal and eternally quotable as the plays or poetry of Shakespeare.

Shakespeare produced the greatest play ever written in *Hamlet*, one in which the alter-ego of his dead son Hamnet is a genius tortured by the murder of his father (Shakespeare typically inverts actual reality, or 'flips the script' in modern parlance, to portray a son mourning his father), who is capable of soliloquising about almost anything. Similarly, Bruce Robinson drew on his own experience of being an out-of-work actor at the end of the 1960s to create the most quotable actor ever, Withnail, and his Boswell (Marwood), who, just like Hamlet, *nail* some of the greatest truths about life, acting and everything in between. And ultimately that is why *Withnail & I* is the closest that cinema gets to having a *Hamlet*.

72 Cond.   72.

> WITHNAIL
> Thou speak-est bollocks. C'mon.

MARWOOD is suddenly on his feet. Retrieves another epee from the
walking-stick tub .. Now he's facing WITHNAIL across the table ..

> MARWOOD
> Alright, Withnail .. Prepare to
> die .. three hits to win .. winner
> buys the drinks ..

Here comes some Errol Flynn - and if it's spelt wrong it's because it's fought wrong .. But these boys can fence - evidentally
part of their drama school training - I'm not going to describe
it because I don't know what it'll look like till we're there ..
But. MARWOOD gets a poke "One" into WITHNAIL's thrattle which
enrages him - fag still burning - he lunges at the coat-hooks
& grabs the mask "Right, you bastard" and the mask goes on ..

The fight continues - WITHNAIL has donned the mask with his cigarette still in his mouth - a thing like a/bee-hive is slashing
around the premises - candles cut. Fuck me! he's picked up a
poker! - but the smoke is still pouring out of the mask - MAR-
WOOD finally wins - WITHNAIL takes "Three" and is down on the
table - point in his neck -"Yield? Yield?" And he does yield ...

AND CUT TO.

73: EXT. LAKESIDE ROAD. NIGHT.   73

WITHNAIL and MARWOOD pound along in the moonlight. A spiteful
wind coming off the lake. Also reflections of a tiny village.
Their destination is one of the few buildings emitting light.

> MARWOOD (V.O)
> *If the Crow & Cunt ever had life it was*
> *dead now. It was like walking into a lung.*
> *A sulphur-stained nicotine-yellow and fly-*
> *blown lung. Its Landlord was a retired al-*
> *coholic with military pretensions and a com-*
> *plexion like the inside of a tea pot. By the*
> *time the doors opened he was arse-holed on*
> *rum and got progressively more arse-holed*
> *till he could take no more and fell over*
> *about twelve o'clock ...*

74

74 INT. 'CROW AND CUNT'. PUBLIC HOUSE. NIGHT.   OUTSIDE THE
                                                                 PHONE BOOTH

A pair of small rooms with a log fire at one end and a bar in
the middle. Thick smoke & packed with men. Mainly Wankers from
the local farms. One or two Shepherds. And one or two apprent-
ice killers previously seen on the march. Everything is yellow
except for the Landlord who is bright red. Years of consistent
boozing have gone into this face. It also has a large moustache.
WITHNAIL and MARWOOD squat on stools at the bar in front of him.

> MARWOOD (V.O.)
> *We took five pints quickly, then moved to*
> *the bar to start on the spirits. The General*
> *had switched to automatic pilot and was now*
> *serving by instinct ...*

```
123 Cond.                                                    123.

                          WITHNAIL (Cond)
              ulties, how like an angel in app-
              rehension, how like a god: ...

         He looks at the wolves in wonder that the bastards aren't clapping.

              the beauty of the world; the par-
              agon of animals; and yet to me,
              what is this quintessence of dust?
              man delights not me, no, nor women,
              neither".. nor women neither ...
                                             &
         Albert Finny never felt so good. He takes a last/final slug at
         the bottle and casts it aside. By Christ, that was the best ren-
         dition of Hamlet the world will ever see! The only pity was it
         was only wolves that saw it. They stare at WITHNAIL through the
         bars. He bids them a silent good-afternoon and walks away ...

         P.O.V. WOLVES. WITHNAIL walks across the park until he is a tiny
         figure in the distance and finally disappears. The MUSIC ends ...

                              THE END
```

The Screen Directions

Appropriately enough for a film in which drinking plays such a large part, at least some of the screen directions in *Withnail & I* are presumably hangovers from the original novel. But regardless of their origin, Bruce Robinson's screen directions were perhaps ultimately the key factor in ensuring that he himself would direct the stunning script that he had written.

Screenwriters are discouraged from writing screen directions because they often contain camera directions, usually considered the exclusive preserve of the eventual director. In the script for *Withnail & I*, however, the screen directions not only provide clues or even instructions as to how the camera should move but vital information about all the other elements of the film-making process, from production design to acting to soundtrack.

For example, Robinson writes in the opening scene: '*Here comes some music… King Curtis on sax … a magnificent rendition of 'A Whiter Shade of Pale' … so sweet … so sour …this is beautiful'*. The words track across the page as the camera will track across the screen, slowly revealing Withnail and Marwood's reality: '*Despite the squalor, the room is furnished with antiques … Objets d'art and breakfast remains compete for space … Dostoyevsky described*

hell as perhaps nothing more than a room with a chair in it. This room has several chairs. A young man sits in one … Now nothing is moving but cigarette smoke. And no sound other than the beautiful lachrymose saxophone.'

This process of providing precise information that is not just about plot or dialogue but about the whole *world* of the film and how it will look and sound continues throughout the screenplay. It even extends to what may be its most important line: the one that sums it all up, in as much as it ever can be summed up. Its importance is not immediately obvious, as Bruce Robinson had hidden it, if not quite in plain view then concealed, as it were, behind a curtain of Latin.

The line is 'A requiem for England', which Withnail says after Monty's pained declaration, 'There can be no true beauty without decay'. In the screenplay, Monty's line is also '*in Latin*', but in the film Richard Griffiths delivers it in English. Withnail's line, however, always remains in Latin and so we, the viewer, remain as much in the dark as Marwood about its meaning when it is delivered.

In modern screenwriting jargon, it is an 'Easter egg', the term for a concealed reference, clue or even inside joke that yields great meaning when it is discovered; in older, 20th-century screenwriting

ABOVE: Excerpt from Bruce Robinson's personal copy of the script.

> **" It touches the moment we've all had when we're all broke, all starving, all aspiring, and all knowing that it might not work in our lives."**

terminology, it is perhaps a 'Rosebud', the one word, or line, that unlocks a script's supposedly secret meaning. But whichever term is applied to it, 'A requiem for England' is the most elegant and eloquent summation within the screenplay itself of what *Withnail & I* is about and why it tugs upon our heartstrings.

It is Withnail's own lament for all that has been lost in his homeland, above all the previously unchallenged economic and cultural dominance that his family and the rest of the English upper class had enjoyed before the economic and cultural earthquake of the 1960s. However, while the Withnails may rue the loss of the 'old order' that they ruled, it is this truly revolutionary period of history that Bruce Robinson himself perhaps lamented.

When *Withnail & I* was released in 1987, Robinson, or perhaps the film's marketers, made much of its recreation of the 1960s, with one early tagline being: '*The 1960s. The greatest party in human history. And Withnail & I are not invited.*' However, as time passed and the Sixties receded in memory, that aspect of the film obviously became less important. Now, nearly forty years on from its release, it is clearer what *Withnail & I* is a requiem for. It is not just England itself (in particular the aristocratic, even ossified, England that the Withnails once ruled), nor the 1960s (that outlier of a decade in which, for the first time, the likes of Bruce Robinson and Marwood could train and work as actors, or musicians, or writers), but Bruce Robinson's own youth, and by extension the whole idea of youth.

Robinson himself perhaps best explained the enduring appeal of *Withnail & I* when he said in the documentary *Withnail and Us* that it 'touches the moment we've all had when we're all broke, all starving, all aspiring, and all knowing that it might not work in our lives'. Actually, Robinson does himself a disservice: *Withnail & I* does not just 'touch' that moment but crystallises it.

And so, in the end, *Withnail & I*, this hilarious film about the alcoholic antics of two out-of-work actors is, in reality, almost the cinematic equivalent of a requiem mass. It may not be as stately or formal as Mozart's or Fauré's actual requiem masses, nor as obviously poetic and nostalgic as Wordsworth's *Ode on Intimations of Immortality from Recollections of Early Childhood*, but it is none

the less a genuinely heartfelt lament for and celebration of all that is gone and all that, in truth, could never endure: old England; the revolutionary spirit of the 1960s; and youth itself.

The Omitted Final Scene

There is one last aspect of the screenplay to consider in order to understand its full effect, namely its original ending, which is perhaps the most famous omitted scene in the history of British cinema. Even though it has never appeared in any of the published versions of the screenplay, it is still widely known by fans of the film and is perhaps crucial to understanding it.

In the earliest drafts of the screenplay, as seen by the likes of Bruce Robinson's friend and fellow screenwriter Andrew Birkin and his eventual director of photography Peter Hannan, the final scene was Withnail returning to the flat that Marwood has vacated and that he will soon be evicted from, pouring the last of the Margaux 53 into both barrels of the shotgun that he has obviously brought back from Crow Crag, and then blowing his brains out in a final, fatal alcoholic 'hit' (in both senses of the word).

It seems that Robinson had every intention of filming this utterly despairing ending, before deciding not to shoot it at all. Presumably he realised that what instead became the final scene – Withnail taking his leave of the wolves and dissolving into the rain to the accompaniment of David Dundas and Rick Wentworth's simultaneously soothing and sinister Wurlitzer-type music – was the *only* possible ending. Rather than definitively killing Withnail off, he left open the possibility that Withnail somehow survived.

In so doing, Robinson allowed for the possibility that his great artistic creation – a modern-day, spectre-thin equivalent of Shakespeare's fat wastrel Falstaff – would live on in the imagination of his audience. And Withnail has emphatically done that, effectively escaping from the pages of a screenplay in which he originally died to become one of the few literary, dramatic and cinematic characters who appear to take on a life, or more precisely an artistic afterlife, of their own. Put simply, Withnail (and by extension I) will never die.

THE SOUNDTRACK

BY NEIL FERGUSON

The movie soundtrack, as a whole, has always been something of an oddity. They're all too often viewed (by the studios at least) as a throwaway product, an afterthought of sorts, frequently reduced to a vomit-inducing smorgasbord of hastily tacked together pop hits *du jour*, an uninspired mess whose sole purpose is simply to push the movie's 'brand'.

There are, of course, honourable exceptions – the likes of John Barry or Ennio Morricone remain true titans of the genre, bona fide musical visionaries who elevated the soundtrack to an art form in itself. Then there are Martin Scorsese and Quentin Tarantino – obsessive auteurs, whose love of popular music informs their work just as much as their reverence for their cinematic forebears. And when movie soundtracks work – when a particular song segues perfectly with a particular scene – they remain a thing of wonder, eliciting a Pavlovian response in the listener, no matter how many times they've been exposed to a particular track. Take Scorsese's *Mean Streets* for example – to this day I can't hear the Stones' sulphurous 'Jumping Jack Flash' without zooming internally to the young De Niro's unhinged, cocksure Johnny Boy, swaggering into a Lower East Side bar with a girl on each arm, in one of the greatest entrances in cinematic history.

This brings us to David Dundas and Rick Wentworth's beautifully curated and oddly eclectic soundtrack to the eternally magnificent *Withnail & I*. An inspired mix of sixties classics, original incidental score, and vintage gems, trigger that same reflexive response. More than thirty years on, I've yet to see Jimi Hendrix used to better effect than in Bruce Robinson's masterpiece. God alone knows how many times I've heard 'Voodoo Chile' but the way it's employed in *Withnail* is downright inspired. To this day, I can be anywhere, in any situation, but just hearing that wah-wah-fuelled intro immediately transports me to Paul McGann's Marwood, blearily coming to in the back of the vintage Jag, only to recoil in abject horror at the sight of a jaundiced-looking, and obviously utterly arseholed, Withnail, sat behind the steering wheel, declaring, with

> **And then he put on that last track 'Withnail's Theme' played on a calliope, which is a little steam organ, and that was it: it was brilliant."**

a certain degree of addled sincerity: 'I'm making time … Here comes another fucker!' as the sound of Hendrix whipping up his own Fender-fuelled apocalypse rages around them.

Likewise, the use of Hendrix' version of 'All Along the Watchtower' – his finest moment on record (this, by the way, is not mere hyperbole. It has been proven by science…) draws the viewer back to the scene where Paul McGann, the very epitome of dishevelled cool, snaps down his shades and pulls the dilapidated old Jaguar out of Camden, a wrecking ball creating havoc in the background as our dysfunctional heroes head off for a delightful weekend in the country. For many fans of The Beatles, 'While My Guitar Gently Weeps' is a) one of the finest tracks on *The White Album* and b) the moment when George Harrison truly came into his own as a songwriter. However, to this listener it exists as

a bitter-sweet exercise in creeping dread, the inner soundtrack to Marwood's hellish stoned paranoia, echoing his unease and tension as he tries desperately to cling onto some semblance of reality while Danny, the demented dope dealer, witters on with drug-addled profundity about the death of the greatest decade known to mankind.

Dundas and Wentworth's incidental score and use of vintage curios, meanwhile, remains an integral part of the film and acts as a kind of counterbalance to the sixties heavyweights. 'Marwood Walks', for example, is one of the most affecting pieces in the entire production, a slight, melancholic slice of pastoral loveliness, a delicate, acoustic inward-looking piece possessing a degree of gorgeous fragility, rather like Marwood himself.

On a purely personal level, it's the music associated with Uncle

OPPOSITE: 'You know, when you first came in, I knew you were a services man.' Photo by Murray Close.

GERARD JOHNSON.
FILM DIRECTOR

I'm always trying to make that perfect London film. A film that captures the essence of that unique city, even though half of it is set in Cumbria, *Withnail & I* gets so much right about London, the people, pubs, streets, cafés, parks, and motorways, this drips authenticity of the late sixties but the genius stroke is stripping it all back.

Now this may have been a choice or a necessity for the budget but who cares? This is how you do it. Iconic isn't easy to pull off. Bruce Robinson literally threw up so much of himself into the celluloid of this picture and for me the personal always makes the best art.

Withnail & I is that perfect London film.

Monty that really resonates. The fruity little piano-driven shuffle of the likes of 'La Fite' or 'Cheval Blanc' to the gorgeous, almost ethereal crooning on Al Bowlly's 'Hang Out the Lights in Indiana' work on so many levels – they're a juxtaposition and counterpoint to the sixties, which is (literally) outside and operating without our titular heroes, and the soundtrack to Monty's inner world, where time has stood still. These are representatives of an entirely different era, a respite of sorts from the booze and drug-soaked lunacy that surrounds them, music that evokes nostalgia and long-lost youth. Monty and, by extension, his music represents refinement, good manners, and a degree of civility (although at a cost), hitherto unimagined by Withnail and Marwood. These pieces create a poignant vacuum where Monty, Marwood, and Withnail are cocooned: 'Perhaps the last island of beauty in the world.'

And finally, we have 'Withnail's Theme', the piece that holds everything together. It's a queasy, lurching minor masterpiece, an odd, haunting fairground ride and with its use of calliope, it echoes, however unintentionally, The Beatles' 1967 exercise in stylised derangement 'Being for the Benefit of Mr. Kite!' It's a pivotal part of *Withnail*, and yet, according to Bruce Robinson in Alistair Owen's

OPPOSITE: Bruce Robinson stunt double in Marwood wig by Sue Love. Photo by Murray Close.

wonderful book *Smoking in Bed: Conversations with Bruce Robinson*, it came about almost by accident rather than design:

'I had terrible problems with the music. David [Dundas] saw the film, I went round to his studio one night, he put it up on the click screen, and my toes were curling, because track after track was completely wrong… he was getting more and more fraught because he could see I didn't like it, and I was getting more and more fraught because I kept saying, 'No, no.' And then he put on that last track 'Withnail's Theme' played on a calliope, which is a little steam organ, and that was it: it was brilliant… he had absolutely one hundred per cent caught the essence of Withnail. So he was delighted and I was delighted, and we just threw all the rest away and that became the focus of the score. It's lovely, and it's haunting and it's memorable.'

And he's absolutely right, Bruce Robinson. It is lovely and it is haunting and it is memorable. It's been 35 years since I first saw and fell utterly in love with *Withnail & I* and its inimitable soundtrack. A soundtrack that remains something of a delightful curio, small but perfectly formed. A thing of slightly deranged beauty and wonder, rather like the film itself.

MATT JOHNSON
SINGER/SONGWRITER

In my opinion, *Withnail & I* is *the* great British film of the 1980s. I first saw it upon its release in 1987. I immediately fell in love with it. One of those few films you want to watch again as soon as it finishes. I've watched it more than a dozen times since. Its depiction of London squat life in the late 1960s put me in mind of my own experiences hanging around dingy London squats in the late 1970s/early 1980s. The best art is always drawn from raw, personal experience, and a lived truth and dark humour permeates the overriding sweet melancholy in nearly every scene. Richard E. Grant and Paul McGann are, of course, mesmerising as a pair of whining misanthropes down on their luck, but then they have a wonderful supporting cast and Bruce Robinson's devilishly

funny script to back them up. A great soundtrack too!`

One of my favourite scenes is when they visit Uncle Monty's run-down farmhouse in the Lake District. You can just feel the cold and damp as the boys shuffle about shivering, hungry, tired and incapable of fending for themselves. Monty shows up a day or so later and, with a wave of his well-manicured hands, transforms the house with the sudden appearance of a roaring log fire, freely flowing wine and a delicious roast dinner. That scene always makes me feel like relocating to the English countryside. There is a monologue from Monty shortly afterwards when the three characters take a walk and he utters the phrase 'kingdom of rains'. I borrowed that line and it became the basis of a song title. There is a little bit of *Withnail & I* in all of us.

RICK WENTWORTH
COMPOSER

Withnail is an odd beast really, because it came and disappeared when it was first released, and after a period of five to ten years it suddenly seemed to grasp the imaginations of so many students in particular. When people discover I co-wrote the score for *Withnail*, they usually start talking about their years at university, and seeing it several times – it's extraordinary. From the moment I was shown the rough cut, which was rough, I thought it was a bloody masterpiece.

Can you remember the first meeting you had with David Dundas about *Withnail*?

We were doing TV commercials, and having considerable success, which I was delighted to be a part of. It was at the time of directors like Ridley and Tony Scott, who graduated from commercials into feature films, so exciting times. The period between '84 through '87, Bruce had become a high profile figure because of *The Killing Fields*. He'd been cited in *The Sunday Times* in one of those lists of people of the next generation who were most likely to succeed, which can be bullshit but in this case turned out to be correct.

Because of David's history, I'd heard about Bruce and read about him – he was this glamorous figure. Out of the blue, David told me Bruce had asked him to work on the score for *Withnail*. I was delighted for him. So it gurgled around in the background while we got on with our day jobs. I would ask him how it was going, and he'd say it was fine, but he was a bit sheepish about it.

David was so close to the reality of those days in the late '60s, living around Bruce and Viv, that I think he was finding it difficult to find a musical vocabulary that would work. This was also Bruce's first film as a director and I suspect he was trying to find his own way around how to musically direct somebody like David, who was also a lifelong friend.

When directors talk about music for films, sometimes it can

be vague, and it's difficult to get a meaningful brief out of them. Bruce talked about Charlie Chaplin and various themes to David. Over the course of a number of weeks, I think David started to begin to get slightly uncomfortable, because every time he played an idea to Bruce, it wasn't met with a tremendous amount of enthusiasm. David discussed it with me and he asked me to join him on the project.

We went into his studio and he played the film, and I immediately took to it – I thought it was extraordinary. And I kept on saying to him: 'This is hilarious.' But I wasn't convinced he felt the same at that moment, I think understandably; detaching himself from the historical reality he knew so well to become objective was very hard.

We reviewed the rough cut and were struggling to know where our input would begin. When you're put up against a great icon like Hendrix and you've got to sit beside it with your work, it's very difficult. The film starts off with a fantastic track from King Curtis, then Hendrix, George Harrison, juxtaposed with music from the 1930s, it's difficult to find a place at that table. It was a challenging palette to figure out what might work.

David and I got to work and started chucking ideas around, then Bruce came over. He was terribly stressed at the time, it was his first film and there was a lot of pressure on him. It was the classic situation where a director can't tell you what they want, but they know when it's wrong.

We had a lot of back and forth, and the reference Bruce always cited was the big theme from the movie *Limelight*. David and I were trying to find something that had that element that we all search for, which has an appropriate atmosphere combined with simplicity, and that's *always* murderously difficult to find. We can all be complicated.

I remember us going out for a curry and it was very late – we'd been working all day. David and I were listening to the background music in the curry house thinking: maybe we can

include a bit of this, and there were tablas and all sorts going on. So we were getting a little bit desperate at that point.

David came into the studio after spending a long night at the piano. He had a theme he'd been developing which he liked. I remember sitting on the sofa with an acoustic guitar and found the opening notes and played some arpeggiated chords around it, and it started to take a shape that seemed to feel we were finally heading somewhere.

Withnail was terrific for me, because this was very early in my career, and I felt very honoured and fortunate to be a part of it. David was generous to include me. It was difficult being the outsider; Bruce and David were very old friends. It felt a little tricky at times; it was difficult to know where one could jump in and suggest things without feeling like an intruder.

That moment of musical collaboration, when the Withnail theme sparked – how did it feel?

It was a great moment; we suddenly felt there was something there. We had a melodic sequence that seemed to be working. And then it became *that* moment where we thought, well, actually, *we* like it; we knew it had possibilities. The calliope sound came from the Emulator. In those days, the 'go-to' keyboards were the DX7 and an E3 Emulator sampler, which was cutting edge.

Speaking with you now, I look back and wonder: did we know we had it at that moment? Well no, not entirely, because the only way we could possibly know that was if Bruce came in and gave the green light.

What about that moment when you first played that to Bruce?

Up to that point, David and I had been through a few meetings with Bruce, and they never really led anywhere specific. We'd spend an hour and a half with Bruce in the studio, at the end of a day, when he was exhausted from the editing process. He was never rude about anything – the opposite, but there wasn't a lot of enthusiasm *until* he heard *that* theme. And suddenly it grabbed him; it was visceral. We were off to the races, because once we had a piece of material that worked – we could vary it and move it around. It was a pivotal moment.

ABOVE: 'I want something's flesh.' Photo by Murray Close.

When you were watching the film rough, do you remember the difficulty of where to start with your music?

It was difficult because Bruce's script is dialogue-led and we didn't want to get in the way; it speaks for itself. When they get to the cottage and Marwood gets up early and goes into the garden alone and the camera pans, showing the beauty of that countryside, we knew that was a place to start, where we had time to establish something.

The particular moment of the soundtrack which I find incredibly haunting and sticks in my mind is the penultimate scene where Marwood is packing to leave; it's just a solo guitar. I'm sure I remember playing that one Saturday morning. I said to John Mackswith – a wonderful engineer who was working with us at the time: 'Let's get a nice sound on the guitar'. David had a Lexicon 224X reverb in the studio, which was a posh bit of kit. We popped that on, and the guitar sounded so wonderful in my headphones. It was an Oscar Teller classical guitar which my father bought for me back in 1964.

To this day that guitar sounds beautiful, particularly when I play that tune on it. One of my daughters picked it up the other day and asked me to play it. It resonates in exactly the same way now and doesn't quite sound like that on any other guitar.

The electric guitar I used, which I still have, was a Roland G808, which was one of the very first guitar synths. I wasn't using the synth module at the time, it was direct into the mixing desk.

What orchestral sound elements did you bring to the collaboration?

We had discussions about maybe making it into a more traditional type of score, where we might have orchestral instruments, but it didn't feel right. When music is put up against a piece of film, there comes a point when it 'sticks' to it, and you know it's right. And if you put a piece of music up that is wrong, it is just *so* wrong.

The great art and skill of music composition for film is precisely that – finding that palette, the level of density, and light and shade that will work for the film. We take it for granted when we see films because it's just there and most of the time you don't

MARGARET CHO
COMEDIAN

Withnail & I is where my Anglophilia and love of drugs intersect, the corner where I live, the cities of my dreams, where I am rarely seen but often see in my wishes. I don't live in England and I don't take drugs, but I have, and I miss it, especially when I watch this film. Although I love it and have since it first appeared in the second run theatre in my hometown of San Francisco in the 1980s, I have never attempted the famous drinking game, where you match characters drink for drink and presumably drug for drug, with or without the lighter fluid (or whatever it is).

If I was a character in this very storied story, I would be one of Danny's clogs, the doll that shits itself, and/or the Camberwell Carrot (no spoilers).

When I went to London in 1994 I could have cared less about Britpop (which disturbs me because now that is all I care about). I spent my time in Camden Town trying to figure out if I would be Withnail or if I was 'I'. What an existential crisis!

I did buy some terrible marijuana from a guy on a bridge who had both his clogs and smoked it in my B&B as the seeds popped away, firing its shrapnel into my eyes. I purchased a PAL copy of it and when I returned home I got it converted to VHS at this British shop in Santa Monica that sold Maltesers and Branston Pickle to those who desperately missed home. I watched different parts of the movie at random when I felt distressed (going to the airport at 3 am, the dentist, auditions, rehab, etc.). It had a soothing effect, much like a Camberwell or lighter fluid or whatever.

> **" For me there was a sense of serendipity. There's that wonderful moment when things come together."**

notice it. And that's how it should be, because the whole business of film composition is a collaborative art form. The mastery of John Williams and so many others sometimes goes unnoticed, which is heart-breaking, but if it was noticed it no longer serves the film. *Withnail & I* is a very modest score in the sense that there isn't a lot of it, but it has a sort of poignancy and works between the diverse amalgam of Jimi Hendrix and period piano music and songs.

What do you remember of creating those '30s soundscapes with La Fite and Cheval Blanc?

We went out of our way to try and emulate that era, and we listened to a whole bunch of stuff. And we made sure that we weren't over-hi-fi-ing it.

When you first saw it in the cinema, and Marwood opens the door of Crow Crag as your music starts – how did you feel?

It was raised hairs on the back of the neck. There's two aspects. There's a bit of: Oh, God. Great, that works. So there's a relief. And then all the technical crap of: Is it up high enough? Or have they pushed it down too far so you can't hear it? But I was delighted. It was a relief to feel we'd done a good job.

How did you feel all these years later, when it was played on Desert Island Discs?

I can't describe how satisfying that was, particularly coming from somebody like Christopher Nolan, for whom I have enormous respect. It was a surprise to hear it and lovely. His kind words resonated in the way I've always thought about it as well. There is a sort of 'rightness' about it.

The sound quality of the dub is pretty appalling by today's standards. We were being told: 'You can't use stereo reverb because it goes right down the middle channel'. There remains though, a certain charm and authenticity about its place in time.

What's your favourite memory of collaborating with David on this soundtrack?

For me there was a sense of serendipity. There's that wonderful moment when things come together. My biggest bloody disappointment is the fact that it came out and for the most part was ignored. Whereas now it's considered a classic, which doesn't surprise me in the slightest. I remember I was struggling with people who were saying: 'Yeah it's all right, but I don't think it's *that* funny.' And I was thinking: Well it must be me then, because I think it's bloody brilliant.

David's generosity to join him on that little adventure was a fantastic moment in my life. It opened doors and experiences that perhaps I wouldn't have had otherwise. I loved the whole process. It was nice to feel I was contributing to something that, in my opinion at that time and now, was very special. Obviously, there were a few hairy moments when it wasn't working, but that's all part of the process.

We had a better understanding of what we wanted to try and achieve once the theme was approved. The calliope and the rising notes for the fairground atmosphere came later, but when it did, it seemed right. When that started to take shape in the studio with Nick Glennie Smith, that was so memorable. There was a moment when I thought: '…this is good'. And it still remains that way when I hear it now.

What do you think it was about Bruce's work on the film that helped make *Withnail* become such a classic?

From this far-distant hill, I can judge it in a way that perhaps I couldn't at the time, but I knew that script was individual, and authentic. I've read that script perhaps more times than I have seen the film in the last thirty years. When one looks at Bruce's scripts for *The Killing Fields* or *Withnail*, there is a unique way of handling the material. *Withnail & I* is such a private, heightened memoir and the material is so personal, that it's hard to imagine it being told adequately by anyone else.

I approached *Withnail* without any preconceptions. I got it immediately because I didn't have any real life reference or memories. To me, these were relatable characters I had come across growing up around the eccentrics of the '60s and '70s.

DAVID DUNDAS
COMPOSER

It was great to see the film again, which I did at the weekend. It all came flooding back. It's such a nice film and it works so well. Watching it again after such a long time reminded me so much of how we started thinking about music for it. We were complete novices. I was used to doing commercials on which Rick and I worked together quite a bit. He's an orchestra man. When Bruce said: 'Listen, you've got to do something for this film,' I freaked out a bit because I hadn't been doing anything which lasted more than two or three minutes. That's when I called Rick in a panic. I thought we needed a professional on board.

I don't think we had a spotting session with Bruce at all. He just said: 'Here's the film, we want you to do the music.' So you sit down and watch it over and over again, and you think: 'Okay, Bruce has put King Curtis' *The Lighter Shade of Pale* on the front, which works brilliantly. Then he's got Jimi Hendrix when the ball hits the building, which is good. But then you get an uncomfortable feeling that you don't know where to come in, because the atmosphere is so good already. And you go through it and you think: 'Where the fuck do we start, and what kind of presence are we when we do start? And eventually we said: 'Okay, let's do something when they come out of the pub, because nothing's happening – they're just running.' Jay Stapely came in and we put in a bit of moody electric guitar with a lot of urban echo which seemed to give the right atmosphere. And once *you're in*, it's kind of okay. But it took us a while to get in.

Bruce told me about that moment when you were playing him things and he was waiting to hear what was in his head…

It was a scary thing, because you don't want to let your friends down, and you know he wants something that he's hearing, but he doesn't know what it is. And *you* don't know what it is. We played him some stuff for when they're trying to catch the fish with a shotgun. And it was just wrong – no good, it wasn't thematic. It was kind of percussive and jumpy and it just didn't do anything. He said: 'Oh God, that's awful.' [Laughs] It was tense that situation. A feeling of impending failure in the air. When he'd left that day, I was thinking: 'I've got to come up with something. I've known him for years. I know what he means, I've got to find it…'

'Sweet and sour, we need a theme and soon,' were the guidelines that Bruce left me with that night, so with a glass of scotch to take the edge off, I played around on the keyboard a bit, shut my eyes, and pretty soon found myself with a little fairgroundy groove that was easy to hum a tune to, and there it was.

In the morning Rick and I put it together with that little calliope fairground organ sound, with Rick playing the tune on one of his many acoustic guitars, (the right one as it happened,) and it felt good. I called Bruce and said 'Come over - I'll play you this thing', thinking: 'He's going to hate this as well.' And he came over and I played it to him, and he said: '*That's it.*' And it's such a nice moment and you think: 'I don't care what happens after this. He's happy.'

When I was watching the movie at the weekend the guitar comes in when they run out of the pub, and you hardly notice it, but it begins to let you in to the movie. They go up to Crow Crag and Marwood comes out in the morning to that solo acoustic guitar – he sniffs the air, the birds are singing, and then we go into that little groove when he opens the gate and walks into the fields, and the theme emerges. We were so happy when we did that and it worked. It had become part of the movie. A new character almost.

What was it like living with Bruce and Viv and the others at Albert Street?

We all came from totally different backgrounds. I went to a public school and it was fine, but I didn't particularly hold on to those friendships afterwards. And therefore meeting people who were

after the same kind of thing, with the same kind of sensibilities, and the same sort of interests and ambitions was *a blast*. I imagine It's like when you go to university, and you find people that you agree with on things and you do stuff together – make little plays and movies and stuff, or whatever project it is. And it was like that – just great.

We were at drama school – a group of people in different flats and rooms in different places. And then gradually, when my father bought this wreck of a house in Camden Town, quite a few people started moving into it. I mean, there were ten of us in there at one stage. The nucleus was Viv, Bruce, me and Mickey Feast, and different people used to come in and out, but that was what it ended up as. It was great – interesting all the time. They were your friends who you understood and wanted to hang out with, and that's what we did for three years.

When did you first read *Withnail & I* and what did you think then?

Bruce gave me a copy, probably when he had the film in place, or maybe earlier. I thought it was great. It was a very familiar story of how it was when Bruce and Viv lived together in the upstairs

flat. It was described as it was. There was the Italian café round the corner and the pub down the road and the feeling of decaying grandeur, and the sink of course. The dialogue is just brilliant. I think even if you're very close to it, you cannot but appreciate the dialogue. Dickensian almost. And the characters: Danny the dealer's way of talking had something of the same atmosphere. Harold Wilson was PM, and there was change in the air. Danny was the one to describe all this. Pearls of wisdom!

When you saw the sink in the film, did you get any bad memories?

Not at all. The period when the sink was out of control was more when Bruce and Viv were there together later on. Mickey and I moved out and went off with our girlfriends. That's when things got rather extreme and unusual upstairs, when Bruce and Viv lived in the flat above. Another old friend of mine lived in the flat below. He had converted it into flats to avoid the sink.

Did you ever worry about the house at that point as you were the landlord?

I was the landlord in that I owned it, but no, I never worried.

ABOVE: David Dundas and Bruce at Crow Crag. Photo by Sophie Robinson.

"As soon as that calliope started he immediately said: 'What's that?' For music writers that's a very important phrase, unless it's uttered with a look of disgust of course."

There's that line in *Withnail* when Danny says: 'Some bald geezer came round for rent' which rather worried me when I first read it, but I was never bald, and I don't think I ever collected any rent as such. Maybe I did sometimes, but no, I didn't worry at all about it. I mean it was a wreck when I bought it, and even more of a wreck when I sold it, and there was a lot of fun and education in between. We were young. You didn't care so much about those things. We lived a fine life on practically no money. It was the 60's.

How well did the film capture that sense of desperation – waiting for an acting role?

I think really well. I mean, the Withnail character is a little bit over the top at times, which is part of the style, and works. But it was very much like that – you'd ring your agent and there was nothing for you, again – particularly Vivian, who was quite a large part of Withnail. And there was jealousy when people went off on acting work. I got a film very early on, and then Bruce got *Romeo and Juliet* very early on with Zeffirelli, and everyone else would get very pissed off and jealous that you were working at all. But then Mickey got a good part in *Hair*, and that was great because we got to know all the guys in the show and they used to come in some nights. I mean the entire cast of *Hair* was in that house sometimes. You'd come in and someone would be in the bath, asleep. It was a happy time.

Can you tell us more about how the collaboration came about with Rick Wentworth? And how did you collaborate on the tracks?

I met Rick when I was doing Channel Four's theme music in 1982. It was very complicated, because for the opening it had to be three and a half minutes long, and had to bring all the regional stations in at different times. I wanted to do an orchestral piece and I didn't know an orchestrator that I rated highly enough. I called Rick because I'd heard some of his stuff – we went for a drink, and got on very well. I asked him to come in on this thing and organize the orchestra, and he did and it was great. I did a ton of commercials in America, and when it was anything using

orchestra Rick would come and do it. He had a lot of success in England too, and still does.

When *Withnail* came along, I immediately got Rick on board as a co-writer so to speak, just for comfort. I didn't know how to do this thing really. If you're together with a mate, you can go through the rough times and spend time working on it, and go out to supper afterwards and talk about it. So it was lovely to have someone else there. *Withnail* was really my thing in terms of putting it together, and the film that Bruce did afterwards which we called '*The Boil*' – Rick did nine-tenths of, so it just depended on what it was, we did things together.

How much did you use the script for inspiration?

Not at all, because we had the movie by then. I think when Bruce gave us the movie, it was locked down. There was no messing around with changes. It was like bringing a new character into a film which was finished, apart from the music. It's a very important part and it's a lot of responsibility and it can get very tense – trying to make sure you've got it right for the director.

Because when you know someone that well it can get tense, and Bruce was suddenly carrying the weight of the whole production. And therefore you're not relying on your 'relaxed giggling, having a pint' kind of relationship. Suddenly things are a lot more serious. Bruce is a strong character, and he wants to get what he wants to get, obviously. I want to get what I want too in a sense, but in that case, I was clearly subservient to him in that I wanted to get it so that he liked it.

How did you develop the synth sounds?

Nick Glennie Smith is a guy who's done a lot of movies, but he used to be a session guy in London who I used a lot with his synth keyboards and amazing musicianship. This was before any kind of digital stuff. I don't think we even had a computer in the studio – everything was live. It was the very early days of synthesizers that could actually sound like real acoustic instruments. I think at the time I had an emulator probably. I used the calliope stop on that. And then when Nick came in, when we were doing the

final theme for the credits at the end, he put on this kind of fairground sound and a string pad. But in those days it was so clearly a synthesizer string pad. You couldn't really create realistic orchestra sounds at that time. Bruce referred to it as 'the organ'.

What made you go for the fairground feel?

Well, I think it evolved because when I was at the piano that night in my studio thinking: 'I've got to find something for Bruce.' It's a bit like acting – you say: 'What is the atmosphere of these guys? It's kind of sad, but it's kind of sweet. And there's this youthful energy…' And then you play around with some chords and hum some stuff over the top and some rhythm, and I remember being very happy with this thing that evolved. The next day I said to Rick: 'You play the tune on the acoustic, and I'll play the calliope. Let's see what it sounds like.' And we recorded that.

When we played it to Bruce, as soon as that calliope started he immediately said: 'What's that?' For music writers that's a very important phrase, unless it's uttered with a look of disgust of course. We said we were working on this piece for some backing, and he latched on to it straight away, because when you've got something like that, you don't have to play the full tune with it. You can just use the: '*Chu-chucka-chucka-chu-cha*' on its own, and Bruce did use it like that. You can pause it; you liven it up a bit. But the time it works best I think is when they don't really know what they're doing up at the cottage. They're kind of wandering around and you just get this: '*Chu-chucka-chucka-chu-cha*,' and then it stops. That's when it worked best. It's like another character watching them.

ABOVE: Paul and Richard in between takes, Cumbria. Photo by Murray Close.

ABOVE: *Withnail* composer David Dundas and Bruce on set at Sleddale Hall. Photo by Sophie Robinson.

What were the recording sessions like and where did you record it?

The recording sessions were at my house. There was no formal recording session as such. I had a Soundcraft desk with a 24-track tape machine. It was very primitive, but perfectly all right. It was the desk that Roger Waters used when he was writing *The Wall*, so it was a desk with some serious history!

How did you get that vintage feel in 'La Fite' and Cheval Blanc?

Ah, how nice that you got onto that. There's obviously something going on with Monty that's not a part of the main theme. Bruce wanted some kind of 50's louche vibe, and I said: 'You know, there are 78 Records I used to listen to when I was ten, and I loved them. There's a guy called Charlie Kunz. He said: 'Have you got any?' I played some Charlie Kunz to Bruce and he said: '*That's it*' again. 'We'll have that', and he used some of that for Monty's flat or Sunday lunch at Crow Crag. And there's a place in the film when they come out of the tea rooms, and get into Monty's ridiculous car and we didn't have anything there. So I said: 'Well, I could do an imitation of Charlie Kunz.' I called a guy called Gerry Butler who I worked with on any piano styles that I couldn't do. I made a tune and said: 'Listen, can you just play that like Charlie Kunz would?' And so there it was. Gerry could play any style you wanted. Another time I played Bruce some Al Bowlly and he put it in somewhere. You have to pay quite a lot for these original tracks and the budget was not huge, so it's often better to use the vibe and record something new. He already had Jimmy Hendrix and King Curtis to deal with.

There was one more bit that I liked when I heard it again, which was when Monty is talking about cycling off with his friend in the old days. I put in a bit of imitation Brahms with a French horn, which I recorded with a piano and a synth backing. It's very soft, but I liked the way that worked too – it does the job. When they're walking in the dark after the pub across the country, it's just a drum machine with a lot of echo, and a bit of electric guitar playing around, and dubbed in quite softly. And it worked fine.

What was the atmosphere like when you visited Crow Crag during the filming?

I think I must have got up there about tea time, or at least drinks-time. There was an air of shock and panic around. Everyone very jittery. I saw Bruce and he was pretty stressed and told me what had happened. They'd obviously had a day shooting in the cottage, and it turned out that Denis O'Brien, (George Harrison's partner,) had actively disliked it, and he'd said: 'I don't know what you're doing. It isn't funny.' I mean, he just didn't get it at all. And therefore everyone's thinking: 'My God, he's going to close us down. We won't have a job tomorrow.' Horrible stress for Bruce. I don't even remember what we did that night. I think we must have just drunk. The next day was a very tense day but Bruce kind of held it together. And we had lunch in a tent outside the cottage, and people just weren't even turning up. They were staying in their caravans. I think if George Harrison had been up there, it wouldn't have happened. But there was a fear that it might be closing down – literally the next day. They'd only done about two scenes.

Knowing Bruce, as you do, could you see Bruce's personality in both the Withnail and Marwood characters?

Certainly in Marwood. There's a time when he puts his dark glasses down when he's driving away in the jag, and he looks quite like Bruce there. So yeah, there are definitely echoes there of Bruce, and also Marwood is writing something all the time and he's got a job, unlike Withnail.

How did you feel when you first saw it at the cinema, and Marwood opens the door to your theme?

Worried, because you always think that it hasn't been dubbed loud enough or too loud, or it's not as clear as it should be in the mix that you had, you know? But happy that it worked.

You saw it again on the weekend – how did you feel about your music all these years later?

I was surprised that it worked so well. I was really pleased with it in fact. A couple of years ago I was in the car coming back from taking my son to school, and Chris Nolan was on *Desert Island Discs*. Suddenly on comes *Marwood Walks* which Nolan was very complimentary about. That was a good moment.

What's your favourite memory of working with Rick on the soundtrack?

When Rick brought his acoustic guitar over to record the theme – it was only him and me. We started off and it just sounded exactly like it should do straight away. And that's a huge contribution to the atmosphere, and that was a very happy moment. As the great Hans Zimmer Says; 'tell the story and get the right player'. When Marwood is leaving at the end – before they go out into Regent's Park, we hear Rick's solo acoustic played freely to picture. That can make or break a scene, and it seemed to me to be exactly right.

MARTIN KESSLER
FILMMAKER

Intrigued by the Ralph Steadman artwork, which graced its cover, I first watched *Withnail & I* not knowing what I was in for. It wasn't even immediately obvious that Bruce Robinson's story of two actor friends who go on vacation – by mistake – was a comedy.

Of course, I'd soon realise that it was absolutely hilarious, but what caught me off-guard and continues to intrigue me about the film is that it doesn't look or feel like a comedy. There's a striking juxtaposition between the fish-out-of-water silliness of the out-of-work actors from the city being out in the country and the captivating gloomy beauty of the countryside that forms the backdrop. Behind the relentlessly funny dialogue, delivered by Paul McGann and Richard E. Grant with pitch-perfect quotability, there's a deep melancholy that resides at the heart of the film. It sticks in the mind like an artefact of dark nostalgia for a not-so-long-ago time that may not have been better days but have certainly been well remembered.

PETER FRAMPTON
MAKEUP ARTIST

What were your thoughts when you first read the script?

Having known the producer and director for some time, I knew it would be wonderfully tongue-in-cheek humour. Also, this was a small film, budget wise, artist wise, and crew wise, and it was nice to be involved in such an 'Ealing type' movie.

Did Bruce give you any additional thoughts on what he envisioned?

Bruce is the nicest and most brilliant man, and any excuse to chat with heads of departments while consuming a crate of wine, to fine-tune the characters, is never missed.

How long did you have to prepare for the film?

Just a couple of weeks. There were no hideous locations to prepare for and this wasn't really period, things like wigs and hairpieces were a doddle.

What did you think of the casting of the film?

Marvellous! Bruce didn't need any heavyweights; in fact, that might have been disastrous.

How did you visualise Danny when you first read the script and when you met Ralph Brown how close did he get to that original vision?

'Danny' was based loosely on a well-known character in the film biz. A hairdresser to be precise and one I have worked with on many occasions.

Can you talk us through Ralph's transformation into Danny?

Ralph's main target was the 'Danny' voice. Anyone in the industry would recognise it immediately. I, of course, designed the tats, which I did by hand each day; apart from eye Kohl and a bad complexion with some dodgy nail varnish… that was that.

What was it like working at Monty's Chelsea pad?

Monty's pad was truly unreal. For a start I lived almost next door and never realised this madhouse was there. There wasn't much need for set dressing, the guy who lived there lived as 'Monty'. We couldn't really show him a script as he would have cut up about being a screaming fag!

What was it like on set up at Crow Crag on that first morning?

Bloody freezing. Because it was virtually on a cliff face, one found oneself walking at a strange angle.

How much research did you do to capture the spirit of '69?

Costume, hair, and I had it nailed because we were all 19 years old at that time – and loved that period… it was ours!

Withnail looked awful after his four-day session – what finishing touches did you add?

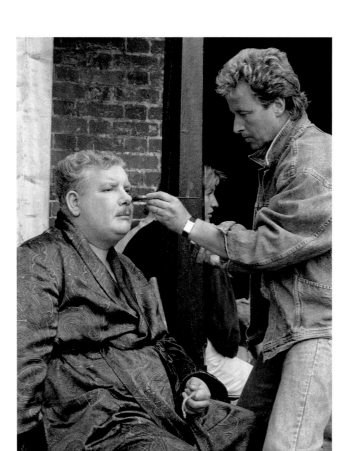

RIGHT: 'He told me about your arrest in the Tottenham Court Road.' Photo by Murray Close.

96

Richard is a makeup artist's dream. Give me half and hour and I'll give you a half-dead 'Withnail'.

Danny's tattoos were spot on – how much work went into those?

I did a camera test on 'Danny' with different tats and Bruce just chose what he liked.

How closely did you work with Sue Love?

We have both worked together for years so again it was a dream.

Did all those rain machines make your life more difficult?

Rain machines are always a bastard!

How nervous were Richard and Paul at the start of filming?

Very. But Bruce being an actor first calmed them down.

What effect did Richard Griffiths's arrival have on the atmosphere on set at Crow Crag?

Brilliant! He was a top man, and so funny.

What was it like working with him?

Utterly wonderful, but he hated being 'camped up'.

Did any of the cast stay in character when getting makeup off?

Maybe Richard E. did a bit, but that's an American habit.

What was your approach to the makeup for Uncle Monty's attempted seduction of Marwood?

I made him up as if he was doing amateur rep – pale foundation, light blue eye shadow, rouged cheeks, and a touch of badly done lipstick.

What did you think when you first watched *Withnail*?

Stunned. Finally a great English comedy after so long.

What was it like working with Bruce Robinson?

It is so hard to find a true gentleman, especially when the director is under such pressure, but Bruce Robinson would be one of the very best… a wonderful guy.

ABOVE: Peter Frampton looks over Marwood's makeup. Photo by Murray Close.

ALISTAIR BARRIE
COMEDIAN AND WRITER

I have just gone through one of the most delightful experiences in British cinema – watching *Withnail & I* for what I believe is technically known as the umpteenth time. It is also the first time I have watched it knowing I was expected to write some sort of essay on it afterwards, not usually something conducive to enhancing one's enjoyment of anything, but in this case, as in so many others, *Withnail* proves itself to be the exception.

Withnail & I is up there in the pantheon of films I have seen so many times I practically know the script off by heart – like *The Wizard of Oz* or *The Sound of Music*, but so much more quotable. It's also in that list of films you find very hard to stop watching once you start – I'd include *Jaws* and *Pulp Fiction* here – because every time you think 'I'd better turn this off and do something productive/go to bed/write an essay,' you also think 'oh, but such and such a scene is next', and it hooks you in again and again until Withnail's last, forlorn walk in the rain as the credits roll.

As a teenager in the Eighties, there were certain films that were, if not exactly ruined, certainly slightly diminished by the fact every other spotty oik you shared a classroom with had already quoted them at you ad nauseam before you'd actually seen them. You were fully aware what the Romans had done for us well before John Cleese actually listed their achievements. Comedy and of course Python were the main culprits here – no-one was surprised when Mr Creosote exploded – and it is interesting to note the connection through HandMade Films and George Harrison, without whom neither *The Life of Brian* nor *Withnail & I* would have been made. Frankly, and excuse the sacrilege, I think I would probably miss them more than I would miss The Beatles.

A lot of the other movies which entered the schoolboy canon were the brilliant US comedies of the 70s, films such as *Animal House*, *Blazing Saddles* and *The Jerk*. A lot of these contained big set-pieces that were easily replicated by young bores, far less funny than they imagined, for each other's amusement – Belushi's

zit, the farting scene, 'I was born a poor black child'. What made *Withnail & I* different was that it was still so eminently quotable, but the appeal was all in the language, the delicious, peerless, indeed unique formulation of words and phrases emanating from the typewriter of Bruce Robinson between glasses of vintage claret. *Withnail & I* has to be one of the wittiest screenplays ever written purely in its exquisite use of language – it is little wonder Robinson was well known for growing irate at anyone improvising around lines he had sweated blood to perfect.

I was very lucky regarding *Withnail & I* in that I came to it relatively fresh and hadn't already had its charms slightly diluted by anyone screaming 'I demand to have some booze' at me repeatedly beforehand. This would of course happen many times in subsequent years – indeed, I would be lying if I didn't admit to being the culprit myself on many more occasions than is advisable, or indeed amusing. I first saw the film just after it had come out on video in 1989 whilst staying at my then girlfriend's house. Back then 'getting a video out' still had a certain mild aura of 'event' about it, something which must seem rather quaint to a generation with the entire artistic output of humanity available to them within a few taps of a smart phone. But this possibly increased the sense of occasion that I still remember, and the feeling of having experienced something genuinely special as Withnail meandered away from the wolves in Regent's Park and that wonderfully emotive theme music started to play.

It is difficult to look on it with a fresh eye now, simply because so many phrases have entered the lexicon, and my mild obsession with the film has led me to not only watching it innumerable times, but reading around it – particularly Richard E. Grant's excellent film diaries, which give a wonderful insight into the casting process and make you yearn to see some of the scenes that ended up on the cutting room floor, like the rapier duel in Crow Crag (yes, really.) But the first thing I noticed this time around was how good the film still looks. It is beautifully filmed and each shot

seems so lovingly framed. Not that I was there, but it really does seem to capture that slightly sepia tone of late 60s Britain – not everything was Carnaby Street/Austin Powers Technicolor, and indeed the brightest thing in Camden Town in 1969 quite possibly *was* the back of the bathroom door in the Withnail flat. Much else was beige, dull and nicotine-stained.

And of course the words. What often strikes me about the film is how simple the structure is – two out of work actors go to the country and come back, The END – but also how, like a great poem, it imbues great slabs of meaning and insight into that structure, and that, surely, is what great art is about. *Withnail & I* is undoubtedly great art. But far more importantly it is FUCKING FUNNY. It is *still* fucking funny, and I was pleased to note how many times I genuinely laughed, over thirty years and countless viewings later. Much of this is down to the two most obviously comic characters, Withnail and Monty, and the delicious lines Robinson gives them, but I do feel Paul McGann deserves a bit more credit than he often receives for playing the straight man so unshowily. His dry narration frames the action beautifully, and I think the main problem is he's just so damned cool in so many shots – the shaving in the bath, flipping down the sunglasses as he sets off in the Jag to *All Along The Watchtower*, strolling around Crow Crag in his leather coat and cap, the green trilby in the final scene. I think that is central to the film's appeal – it's pretty tricky to be cool and funny at the same time, but *Withnail & I* is such a stylish film, with McGann's obvious yet slightly naive sexiness, but also Withnail's Savile row suit, Monty's Rolls, the beat-up Jag, hell, even Monty's radish buttonhole. And the music. There is a whole different essay to be written on the music, but like much

else in the film, it is the fact it is used so sparingly that makes its use so devastating – from the hugely atmospheric *Whiter Shade of Pale* that soundtracks the opening montage to the wrenching use of *Voodoo Chile* kicking in as they career down the motorway back to London ('I'M MAKING TIME!'), all underlined throughout by the brilliantly minimalist and eventually almost heartbreaking Withnail theme.

The performances are all universally excellent. Of course, special mention must go to Richard E. Grant whose splenetic, permanently unwell Withnail is one of cinema's great creations. As evidenced by his clear delight at his relatively recent Oscar® nomination, Grant obviously can't believe his luck and has always been disarmingly honest about both what a gift this part was and how it essentially paved the way for every success he has had since. As an actor you have to grab a gift, and he does so with both hands and such wild abandon that you are carried away by both his enthusiasm and the occasional flashes of pathos he allows you to glimpse behind those mad, rheumy eyes. But most of the time he is having so much fun, we cannot help ourselves but join him. It is not without good reason his words have now joined those ranks of the most quoted in British comedy history.

For me, though, it will always be Monty (you terrible cunt). Richard Griffiths packs more into his relatively small part here

TOP LEFT: 'The carrot has mystery. Flowers are essentially tarts.'

ABOVE RIGHT: 'Oh, Baudelaire. Brings back such memories of Oxford.' Richard Griffiths OBE passed away on 28th March 2013. Photo by Murray Close.

than most actors do in an entire career. From his pronunciation of 'thez-bian' in the first scene to his monologue on never playing the Dane, there is not a word, an action or an eyebrow out of place. Much of what he says retains a wonderful universal quality – I'm not sure Monty would have been a Brexiteer, but much of his harking back to glorious bygone days would surely resonate with that demographic – which is surely another key to its longevity and status. Who can fail to love a line like,

We live in a land of weather forecasts and breakfasts that set in. Shat on by Tories, shovelled up by Labour...'

I mean – 'breakfasts that set in?' How do you even come up with that!? It's utterly glorious and Griffiths gives it everything. I still cannot walk through 'beastly mud and oomska' without remarking on it, and the sky will always begin to bruise and we will be forced to camp. (I suppose what I'm saying here is it's probably best not to go for a walk with me in the rain.)

A debate I always enjoy is over who is the best supporting character in *Blackadder* (another entry for the massively over-quoted world championships, and I'm afraid to say I know *every* word). While I will never think of Hugh Laurie's George(s) as anything but a work of comedic genius, it is always Tim McInnerny's Percy from series 2 who will carry the day for me, somehow managing to convey so much more than just pant-wetting hilarity. I can pay Richard Griffiths no greater compliment than to say I simply could not choose between Monty and Percy for my absolute favourite of all time, and thankfully, as they operate in slightly different genres, I don't have to.

Withnail & I has been a constant friend to me for over thirty years now, and I couldn't really imagine life without it – it would be like doing away with *Blackadder*, with *Jaws*, with Python, with all those books and songs and plays and poems that provide you with that essential enjoyment, yet also that examination of humanity, which is what culture and ultimately life itself is all about. I was appalled recently when a friend in his twenties hadn't even heard of it. It was a bit like finding yourself in that

Richard Curtis film where The Beatles never existed. (Could I make it quite clear I am very happy The Beatles existed? It's just I happen to have mentioned their non-existence twice now and I'd hate anybody to get the wrong idea.) Similarly, I was having a drink with a member of staff at the comedy club I was playing this weekend who had never read *The Hitchhiker's Guide to The Galaxy*, so that was a trip to Waterstones on Saturday morning as we can't have that sort of ignorance going around in our young people untreated. My boys, my boys...

I described *Withnail & I* earlier as 'great art', which might seem quite a high-blown claim for a film which is essentially a few days in the life of a couple of pissed actors, but then pissed actors might be quite a decent way to describe humanity, and Withnail and Marwood are in a sense Vladimir and Estragon waiting for their very own Godot. The film's tragedy is of course that at its conclusion Withnail watches Marwood find his while he remains, still waiting, perhaps permanently.

I too was a little lost as to how I might conclude this piece, but then something rather lovely happened as I watched the film. I watched it on YouTube – the fact it is available there in full probably further proof of Bruce Robinson's somewhat upsetting claim he never made a penny out of it – and the version I saw had subtitles. This meant that for the first time I understood one of the jokes I have never got before, mainly because, as Peter Cook once said, I never had the Latin. As the three of them are sat round the table at the cottage playing cards, Monty remarks to Withnail, ostensibly about a card that has been dealt , 'Looking a bit lonely, isn't he?' To which Withnail replies (also in Latin) 'He needs a Queen to come to the rescue,' leaving Marwood looking exquisitely uncomfortable as they both collapse into giggles.

I did too. It is surely the mark of great art that you keep discovering more within it every time you return to it. And I will be going back to *Withnail & I* time and again, hopefully for another thirty years. The old order may well changeth, yielding place to new. But classics are classics for a reason, like ice in the cider. And you can quote me on that.

OPPOSITE: 'And here we are, we three, perhaps the last island of beauty in the world.' Photo by Murray Close.

MURRAY CLOSE
STILL PHOTOGRAPHER

How did you get to work on the *Withnail* project?

I came to it via a strange route, in that I started my career with Warner Brothers with Stanley Kubrick's *The Shining*. At that time they distributed HandMade and said: 'HandMade have got this little film, before you start on *The Little Shop of Horrors*, can you do us a favour? We want to make sure we get some good photos.' HandMade couldn't afford me every day, so I tried to be there for all the crucial scenes. I was only there for maybe 12 days in total.

What was your first meeting with Bruce Robinson like and what was his brief to you?

The first meeting with Bruce was on set when they were fishing in the river with the shotgun. It was like a film school production in some ways, because there were no big stars in it. And no one had huge egos. Bruce had never directed before. It was just so casual. It was mainly all the HandMade crew like Clive Winter on sound, Peter Hannan as DP, Peter Frampton on makeup and Peter Kohn as assistant director, so there were some faces I knew.

Bruce's hands were obviously so full; I think the last thing in the world he was thinking of was any sort of publicity campaign or any particular images he wanted me to catch. He just trusted me to do what I do well. It was a lovely atmosphere. It was very convivial – in the sense that there was no pecking order or people going off to their trailers – they didn't have trailers. Everyone just sat on the grass in between shots. If I wanted a bit of time to take photographs of the actors, I grabbed them. It was very English, everyone was charming. There were no bad tempers. Everyone had some beers at night together. It was like a big adventure. What we did know was that the script was bloody brilliant. Oh man, that script was amazing, and still is.

What was the atmosphere like on the first day of filming at the Notting Hill location?

Well, it was chaos. Whenever you try and shoot a film in a real location, and you're trying to get 50 people in a small room, it always is. The only room that was really workable was the living room area, because you can move things around a little bit. I mean, everything was practical. That was a real kitchen, and a real bathroom. It wasn't movie-friendly – it was like a former squat. That area was a shithole – it wasn't fancy at all. I used to hang out down there to see bands like Hawkwind near the Westway, so I knew that area well and it was not nice – nowhere near like it is now. We all wish we bought properties there in the early '80s.

When did you get your chance to photograph Ralph Brown as Danny?

There was a scene when he's just woken up – lying on the bed and the Camberwell carrot scene. I don't think at the time anyone realised how famous his character was going to become. By the time he put that twist on the accent, I do wonder if Bruce wishes he shot some more scenes with Danny. He's become disproportionately one of the main stars when you consider the amount of scenes he shot.

What was your main aim when capturing the images during filming?

Obviously I was there to document the scenes, in particular those that we all thought were going to be the most photogenic. The shots in the flat were tricky photographically; those images are less interesting to me. In terms of strong images, there's Monty's cottage and Regent's Park, and the tea room – a classic.

What are your memories of Richard corpsing during that Tea Room scene?

People do talk about that a lot, but for me I think it was Paul that was corpsing more. Richard was giggling, but it was Paul that was shoving food in his mouth because he was about to break character. The tea room and the Wellington boots scenes we did in

ABOVE: 'The police, Miss Blennerhassett.' Photos by Murray Close.

a single day, so there was no time to muck about. I nicknamed the photo with Richard Griffiths and the car 'Booze or boots?'

Bruce wanted very low light levels. How did you deal with that?

It was tricky those days – tricky for me to handle because I had to force-develop the film. Black and white was easier. For colour, it was slides and positives in those days. It's tricky to look at some of the interior shots in Monty's place because in some of those interior images the contrast gets built up as you're force-developing something. So compared with what we get now, it's not good. That's why all the black and white images really make up my *Withnail* portfolio. Some people still think the film was shot in black and white. We used Arriflex cameras because they were cheap, but they were noisier than Panavision cameras, so we used to use Peter Kohn's very expensive leather jacket to cover the camera just to make it quiet. We called it the Armani Barney. Technically it was tricky, there's no two ways about that.

Crazily I didn't shoot much really. I don't recall being given a brief like: 'Go easy', but I got what I thought was enough, and compared with the amount of material that I would shoot now it was a mere fraction.

You must have had to squeeze into some tight spaces to stay out the way. Which scene did you find most difficult to stay close to the action?

It was probably the lunch scene in Monty's cottage: 'And here we are, we three'. I was jammed in at the end of the dining room table. You'd end up sitting on each other's laps. When Paul's almost naked when Monty's coming upstairs, I shot that, and that room upstairs was minuscule. That's one of the downsides of using a practical location.

We did some of that scene near Rickmansworth, where we did the pub with the General and Michael Elphick when they all get drunk. It was all done on the cheap – there was absolutely no money.

> **"With Bruce it's obviously all about the words. It starts with the words and then the actors."**

Were there any issues keeping the wolves interested?

Yeah, I think the prop guys had some sort of snack. From what I remember, we were just operating as a guerrilla unit. I don't think we had the help of London Zoo – I think we were just winging it. We shot the walk and talk through the park and the soliloquy scene in a single day.

What do you think of Peter Hannan's work on the film?

Peter had a very good sense of humour. Australian DPs are very practical, like John Seale, Dean Semler, and Peter – all those guys when they broke into Europe or America. They're very practical because the films that they grew up making in Australia had zero money as well. So they knew how to make things work without much money. They weren't like big fancy American DPs who had loads of gear. They knew how to do it dirty and make it look nice. Pete was one of those guys. I subsequently worked with him on *Prisoner of Azkaban*. Peter's a great guy.

Sadly, the camera operator Bob Smith died – Smudger Smith. Bob was absolutely essential to Bruce. He'd tell Bruce what we needed to make the scene work.

When did you first notice it becoming a cult?

It couldn't really become cult until the Criterion Collection got the DVD rights. I had an old VHS copy of it, and that thing was worn ragged, because I'd been constantly lending it to people.

With all the shenanigans with HandMade films, you couldn't get it on video for years. And then Criterion got the rights when I was living in LA in '96.

Suddenly people could see it again, and then it took off, but it had lain in the doldrums for ten years. You might have got a midnight screening at one of the Soho movie theatres, but everyone had walked away from it. It wasn't a hit. HandMade were folded up. It was just done, it was over. It was a great project. Everyone enjoyed it, it was fun, but that was it. It was sort of revisionist history.

What was the most stressful moment during filming?

I don't recall any atmosphere like that. Everyone was cool. Pete Kohn, his style of assisting wasn't shouting, he'd just be cool – trying to sort any problems out. Bruce obviously had his moments with the producer talking to HandMade when they wanted to shut things down, and I'm sure there were some pretty tense moments there. But actually on set everyone was charming. I can't think of one weird situation. It was a lovely experience. But immediately after it finished we all went on to bigger things, of course.

We had a screening at BAFTA. I think George Harrison came to that. And we all got together then. David Wimbury's nickname was Petal, and he gave us a few of these great hip flasks with the Ralph Steadman lettering and on the back:

GWBFM

THE AUDIENCE

PAUL WEBB,

MUSICIAN

I always get excited when I come across people who've never seen this before, because it gives me the perfect excuse to sit them down and watch this joyful story unfold itself all over again. *Withnail & I* is just as potently funny and entertaining now as it ever was, making it easily my favourite British comedy film of all time.

Which was an acronym for the Guild of Whinging British Film Makers. He said that us lot were always moaning the food wasn't any good and what have you, so he passed these around. He was a lovely bloke, Petal – he was smashing.

How tricky was it dealing with the rain machines with camera in hand?

We were used to that, no problem. In those days, you'd have to put these boxes around the cameras to deaden the noise of it. By the time you'd put a carrier bag over that as well, it was fine. It was ugly and it was clumsy but it sort of worked. You'd get more of an issue with the lens steaming up.

What happened when filming ended after the soliloquy in Regent's Park?

It was raining, and I think the light was probably going. It was a Sunday. I think we all went over to the York & Albany to have some beers afterwards. That pub was a shithole in those days but now it's a posh gastropub.

What happened when Ringo showed up on set?

No one was expecting him to show up. I got the feeling there may have been some sort of private thing, so that Ringo had to be in the country or show he was involved in the project. It seemed to have nothing to do with film. He came down and hung out and I took a picture of him, Paul, and Bruce together – it was in the Notting Hill location.

What is your own personal favourite *Withnail & I* photo?

Personally, the one I like most I call 'adieu', which shows the top of Paul's head in the hat walking away from Withnail in the rain. I mean, all my personal favourites are black and white. I hardly have any of the colour ones – HandMade lost most the colour images, I kept all the black and white – that was my deal. I've been the guardian of the black and white images in particular, although I do have some colour ones.

Which print gets bought most often?

'Booze or boots?' is pretty popular, funnily enough, because it has all three of them, and one of the tea room picture is very popular, but the biggest seller is 'Natural Theatre', when he's up in the Lake District with his back to camera and shouts: 'I'm going to be a star.'

How would you describe Bruce's approach to directing?

With Bruce it's obviously all about the words. It starts with the words and then the actors, whereas I get the impression the

technical side of things is not where he gets the most enjoyment. He would rehearse with the actors before we got the cameras out. He had very specific ways that he wanted the scene to go. And, in fact, I don't think there were any changes in the script, and I don't recall any ad libs, yet in modern-day comedies the actors are constantly ad-libbing.

I don't even think *Withnail & I* is even a comedy. It's a love story between two friends, and not in a sexual way at all. There are no women in the thing, except for Miss Blennerhassett, the farmer's mother, the scrubbers, and the woman eating the egg sandwich. It's so hard to pigeonhole the film.

TOP: Richard E. Grant, Paul McGann, Ringo Starr.

ABOVE: 'And yet, to me, what is this quintessence of dust? Man delights not me — no, nor women neither, nor women neither.' Withnail & I, Regents Park. Photo by Murray Close.

CHARLIE HIGSON

WRITER, ACTOR, COMEDIAN

unnily enough (or not funnily at all, actually), for a country that creates so much comedy, and for whose population humour is such an important part of their lives, we Brits make surprisingly few great comedy films. All that energy seems to have been channelled more into TV and stand-up rather than cinema. And British comedy films have tended to be small-scale, inward-looking, about focusing on character and class and social embarrassment.

Back in the day, there was Will Hay (but who watches Will Hay films today?), and the parochial delights of Gracie Fields, Norman Wisdom and George Formby... Old Mother Riley, anyone? Ealing Studios made a few good comedies, the standouts being *The Ladykillers* and *Kind Hearts and Coronets*. *Private's Progress* and *I'm All Right Jack*, were made by The Boulting Brothers, who had their own ensemble team to rival Ealing – featuring the likes of Peter Sellers, Ian Carmichael and Terry Thomas – who, along with Alistair Sim and George Cole shone some comedy light into the 50s and 60s through films like *School for Scoundrels* and *Laughter in Paradise*. Things woke up a little in the 60s with some more up-to-date comedies, like the Beatles films, *The Knack*, *Billy Liar*, *Alfie* and *Dr Strangelove*, but mostly the cinemas were full of long-running series like *St Trinian's*, the *Doctor* films and the *Carry On* films.

Carry On peaked in the '70s, which was a wasteland of unnecessary TV sitcom spin-offs and sex comedies, saved only by the Pink Panther and Python, with the wonderful *Holy Grail* and *Life of Brian*.

And there were slim pickings in the '80s; the best offerings were probably *Gregory's Girl*, *A Fish Called Wanda*, *A Private Function*, *Rita, Sue and Bob Too*, *Educating Rita* and *Shirley Valentine* (the last three of which were based on plays); but head and shoulders above all of them was an outlier, a film that seemed to come from nowhere – *Withnail & I*. Not just a great comedy, it was a great film and very different to anything else around at

the time, even though, like all the other films mentioned, it has that very British, parochial, inward-looking, class-conscious and character-based feel about it. Coming from a very different place to the more riotous American fare of the time – John Hughes, *Airplane*, *Ghostbusters*, Eddie Murphy, Chevy Chase – *Withnail* wasn't a hit on release but has had a long and illustrious afterlife through DVDs and online, where its popularity has kept on growing. And, crucially, I think a huge amount of subsequent British comedy had some of its roots, whether consciously or not, in Bruce Robinson's film. It was one of the first examples of the bromantic comedy, where two mismatched men go on a road trip and spar with each other. The characters of 'Steve Coogan' and 'Rob Brydon' in the series *The Trip* could be the children of *Withnail & I*. And the film showed very clearly that we could all take to heart a comedy character who was not necessarily cute and superficially lovable (see Alan Partridge, Loadsamoney, The Only Gay In The Village, etc.) Through its dialogue, the film's colourful, liberal and creative use of swearing paved the way for many other misanthropic fuckers since, like Malcolm Tucker and Jeremy and Mark in *Peep Show*. Simon Pegg and Edgar Wright have both spoken about how much they love the film, and how it fed into their own work, in particular *Hot Fuzz*, with its celebration of small-scale Britishness and its town vs. country aesthetic. And the film's gloomy, grey, rain-soaked, northern, Gothic atmosphere surely had an influence on *The League of Gentlemen*. The scene in the Penrith Tea Rooms, with 'Mabs' and the outraged cravat-wearing proprietor, always reminds me of Tubbs and Edward in their local shop for local people.

I know that *I* was definitely influenced by the film. I was starting to write comedy with Paul Whitehouse at the time it was released, and we immediately added it to our list of touchstones – work that we both loved and wanted to emulate – our own set texts for the creation of memorable characters and great dialogue – from *Bedazzled* through *Life of Brian* to *This Is Spinal Tap* and

Mike Leigh's *Nuts in May* via *Get Carter* (not a comedy film, as such, but packed with great lines and blackly/bleakly comic scenes). Bruce Robinson (at least with this film) joined the likes of Clement and La Frenais, Galton and Simpson, and Croft and Perry on our list of greats.

Not all of our influences were necessarily so classy. It was hard to escape the more mainstream comedy of Dick Emery and *Carry On*, both of which, like so much of the comedy we'd grown up on, came out of the strong tradition of character comedy in British Music Hall.

The character comedy work in *Withnail* is exquisite. In the end, it's much more about character than plot (there are many funny incidents – the bull, the urine sample, the chicken – but no great comedy arc to the film). There's not a dull or make-weight character in it. The deluded, ranting Withnail, the more introverted and thoughtful Marwood (as 'I' is called in the script), appalled at the world and wondering if he'll ever get anywhere in it. The disgraceful, yet still lovable, Uncle Monty (based on several

predatory older men that Robinson had had to deal with as a beautiful young actor, particularly the Italian film director Franco Zeffirelli), and Danny the dealer, with his Camberwell Carrot (which has entered the public lexicon).

I give a lot of advice to aspiring screenwriters, as well as teaching occasional classes and workshops, and I always advise my students to read existing scripts, adding that one of the best is Bruce Robinson's script for *Withnail & I* (available from Bloomsbury). It's a beautifully written piece of work and everything that's great in the film is there on the page. Reading it again, as I did before writing this piece, makes you want to instantly go back and watch the film again one more time.

In many ways the script is all wrong. It doesn't follow the rules, and the film shouldn't work. There's no standard structure to it, things just unfold. You keep thinking – *yeah I love this bit* – and then something else comes along and you think – *oh God, yeah, I'd forgotten this bit, there's still loads to come…* More comic scenes, more fantastic dialogue. It's picaresque, episodic, and rambling,

ABOVE: 'Sherry?'
Photo by Murray
Close.

although it gradually and subtly builds towards a surprisingly emotional ending, with its death of friendship.

But it's the unconventional nature of the film that makes it so endlessly rewatchable. There's no Hollywood machine pressing all your buttons in all the prescribed places, making sure all the dramatic and emotional beats hit with tedious, metronomic and mathematical precision. The same in every film, whether it's a comedy, a drama, a kids' cartoon, or a fantasy epic.

What's particularly striking about the script is that it's so *readable*. A good script shouldn't just be a collection of bland stage directions interspersed with chunks of dialogue; it should portray the essence of the film. It should bring to life its atmosphere and conjure up in the reader the experience of watching it (without telling the director what to do). To do that without writing reams of description (which readers tend to skip through anyway) is a real art. If you overdo it, it's tedious, but, when you get it right, as Bruce Robinson did, it sings.

It has to be said that most film scripts, even those from great films, are not a great reading experience. But there's an element of poetry to the script for *Withnail* – just as there is in the finished film – and there's an impressionistic feel as well, with carefully chosen words painting a vivid picture. Robinson creates a complete, vivid world that you become immersed in. This is crucial, because the atmosphere and the settings are almost as important and memorable as the characters, and are such a huge part of its long-lasting appeal. Reading the script, you live in that

grotty Camden Town flat with its ruined grandeur, you hang out in Monty's luxuriously decaying, bohemian Chelsea pad and travel to the god-awful, and even more decaying, farmhouse in Cumbria. You feel the cold and damp and the grey misery of the late '60s and early '70s, you feel the menace from the various men our two perfumed ponce heroes have to deal with.

Right from page one, you're there and you're gripped, and you want to read on…

'Dostoyevsky described hell as perhaps nothing more than a room with a chair in it. This room has several chairs. A young man sits in one. He isn't comfortable. He is leaning forward. He is scrutinising his thumbs. He is wired. Now he's lighting a cigarette. Now nothing is moving but cigarette smoke […] The man in the chair is Marwood. 25 years old. Milk white with insomnia. Glasses like Lennon's and a sweet face behind them. 75% good looks and the rest is anxiety. This is a long haul with unspecified destination […]

And everything looks ill. The walls and furniture look ill. Daylight looks ill…'

What's extraordinary is how close it all is to the finished product. Obviously, it helped that Robinson was able to direct it as well as write it, but even so, usually, with even the best scripts, a great deal changes from page to screen. Robinson had worked on it for over fifteen years when he came to shoot it, so he'd had time to get it right, but often a long creative process can lead to things becoming over-worked and stale. The script for *Withnail* feels brilliantly alive – if rather fetid and sick.

And then there's the dialogue. Every line works, character and speech perfectly married, and almost every line quotable (as Richard E. Grant demonstrated in 2020 with his popular string of tweets from around the world recreating his most famous lines). Crucially, they grow out of the characters; Robinson doesn't just stuff words into characters' mouths willy-nilly. They all have their own distinct speech patterns. Marwood quiet and introspective, Withnail ranting, Monty poetic. We never get the feeling that this is just Robinson talking (in the way that you can, for instance, always hear Woody Allen speaking through his characters).

'I must have some booze. I demand to have some booze!'

'Oh, my boys, my boys, we are at the end of an age! We live in a land of weather forecasts and breakfasts that 'set in', shat on by Tories, shovelled up by Labour, and here we are. We three. Perhaps the last island of beauty in the world.'

'I often wonder where Norman is now. Probably wintering with his mother in Guildford. A cat and rain. Vim under the sink. And both bars on. But old now. There is no beauty without decay.'

'How dare you? How dare you? How dare you call me inhumane?'

'Listen to me, listen to me. There are things in there, there's a tea-bag growing. You haven't slept in sixty hours you're in no state to tackle it. Wait till the morning, we'll go in together.'

'This is the morning. Stand aside!'

'There's something floating up.'

'Fork it!'

'Have we got any embrocation?'

'What for?'

'To rub on us, you fool. We can cover ourselves in Deep Heat and get up against the radiator. Keep ourselves alive until twelve.'

'I must have some booze. I demand to have some booze. What's in your toolbox?'

'We have nothing. Sit down.'

'Liar. You've got antifreeze.'

'You bloody fool you should never mix your drinks!'

'We want the finest wines available to humanity! We want them here and we want them now!'

'I feel like a pig shat in my head.'

'I don't advise a haircut, man. All hairdressers are in the employment of the government. Hairs are your aerials. They pick up signals from the cosmos and transmit them directly into your brain! This is the reason

bald-headed men are uptight.'

'Are you the farmer? We've gone on holiday by mistake.'

And possibly the greatest line of all time...

'Monty, you terrible cunt!'

It's all there on the page – mood, character, setting, humour, tone. And you really want to keep reading. And I can tell you from thirty years of reading scripts that that is by no means always the case. In his excellent book *With Nails: The Film Diaries of Richard E. Grant*, the actor shows us what he felt on first reading all this...

'Two pages into the script and an ache has developed in my gonads – I am both laughing out loud and agonized by the fact that the Withnail part is such a corker that not in a billion bank holidays will they ever seriously consider me...'

When you read the script yourself, you can see just why he was excited. And what a great first appearance his character has. Equally as vivid and telling as the description of Marwood above...

'30 years old. Pale as an oven ready chicken. His hair is wet. The eyes have practically vanished under mauve lids. But the face is shaved and has dignity. So do the clothes. He wears a tweed overcoat. Corduroy trousers and brogues. There's class here somewhere. His name is Withnail.

WITHNAIL: I have some extremely distressing news...'

Reading the script today, it's impossible to imagine anyone else in the three lead roles. The film is a magical synthesis of script and actor being perfectly matched. Reading the diary that Richard E. Grant kept at the time it's clear that many other actors were up for both lead roles, and you read it wanting to shout out, 'No, you can't cast them!'. They're all good actors, they're just not as perfect as Richard E. Grant and Paul McGann. And you know the film would have suffered (just as *Casablanca* would have suffered if they'd insisted on keeping the lead actor it was originally written for – Ronald Reagan).

Paul McGann has that wonderful beauty and soulfulness

and is very self-contained. There's always something slightly hidden about him, something unknowable. And the fact that, as a Liverpudlian, he wasn't using his own accent makes him hard to pin down. Withnail shows everything on the outside. He batters himself against everyone and everything but he can't ever fully get through to Marwood, and, in the end, is left abandoned.

Grant and Withnail are inseparable. What a way to burn yourself into the public consciousness. What a role. A role for which he was so perfect that he can perhaps never escape from it. It's almost impossible to believe that Grant wasn't a drinker and had to see what it was like to get drunk before filming and then vow never again. In his book, he describes himself as relentless, and so is Withnail. He has that wide-eyed, appalled innocence and affront at the world. Withnail comes from that long list of fantastic characters who are mesmerising on screen, but who you wouldn't want to get stuck with in real life. I love Richard E. Grant's acting, which is why I was so happy when he agreed to play a key role in my *Jekyll and Hyde* TV series. He's an actor who's not afraid to go for it, just as Withnail is a character who's not afraid to go for it.

This could only be a British film. The fact that it doesn't follow the classic Hollywood line, hitting all the buttons in the same places as every other film they've ever made, makes it so rewatchable. You're not constantly made aware of being manipulated, of having your levers pulled and having false emotions forced on you. The script just unfolds, and we are spectators of these young men's lives. Free to draw our own conclusions. We watch their friendship grow, then fracture, and then dissolve. We know that Marwood is going to be a star and we know that Withnail never is. His only audience will be the wolves – and *us*, standing in the wolves' enclosure looking out – and applauding.

'**By Christ that was the best rendition of *Hamlet* the world will ever see! The only pity was it was only wolves that saw it. They stare at Withnail through the bars. He bids them a silent good afternoon and walks away.**

POV wolves: Withnail walks across the park until he is a tiny figure in the distance. The sweet and sour music rises into appropriate orchestral perfection as he finally, and far away, disappears.'

ABOVE: 'Monty, you terrible cunt!' Photo by Murray Close.

DEAN CAMERON

ACTOR, DIRECTOR

I've always thought that the best movies are the ones that give you a glimpse into a world that you didn't know existed. Or alien subcultures. *Animal House*, *Apocalypse Now*, *The Godfather*, and *Lawrence of Arabia* all create worlds and characters that, after watching, you can say 'I was there. I know exactly what it was like.' You feel as if you are an authority on the subject because you've lived the experience.

When *Withnail & I* is over, you've been an unemployed actor in London at the end of the sixties.

For me, the movie is, ultimately, a tragedy. It's incredibly sad. 'I' loves Withnail so much but by the end understands that he can't be friends anymore – he has to save himself. Withnail is one of those mad genius friends who are so much fun to be around but you know that another weekend with them will kill you. When the first *Jackass* movie came out, I told my wife: 'That was a documentary about being a guy and having a best friend.' You love each other so damned much, and, instead of having sex, you beat the shit out of each other or go on mad adventures.

There is also a truth about showbiz friendships that is drawn so beautifully. 'I' recognizes Withnail's genius and has been along for the 'We geniuses are unemployed because those bastards don't know that we're geniuses, dammit and reject their horrible show business!!!' ride. They've both believed that it is Withnail who will be the success. It is Withnail who will drop the ladder down to 'I' once Withnail becomes the toast of the theatrical world. And yet, it is 'I' who gets the gig. The unspoken agreement… the ending of the 'script' they've written and agreed on has completely changed. Reality is here. It's time to grow up and move on.

Richard E. Grant is a phenomenon. As a young actor in the 80s when *Withnail & I* came out, everyone was longing for a role like that – a mad, ballistic role that would jump off the screen. I continue to long for one. However, only a few years ago, after someone pointed out to me that it was Tom Cruise who had the difficult role in *Rain Man*, I realised that Paul McGann was the

actor doing the real heavy lifting in *Withnail & I*. Acting is reacting, after all…

But the lesson to be learned from that is you stay the course and you'll end up as Doctor Who and doing cool stuff that may not be as fantastic, but you work. Maybe you don't get the lead in the Spice Girls movie or *How to Get Ahead in Advertising* but maybe you end up as a Doctor Who. There are many roads and being a tenacious working actor with longevity is the ultimate goal.

The other characters – Monty, Danny, whatever the fuck is in the sink at the beginning, the person eating the awful egg sandwich and, of course, the unforgiving, wet, and claustrophobic British winter. They're all conspiring against Withnail & I. Withnail is probably destroyed, right? 'I' is telling the story.

There are two movies that end with looks that haunt me. *The Graduate* – the look of Katharine Ross and Dustin Hoffman of 'Uh-oh… what now?' and *Withnail & I* with Richard E. Grant's monologue. Brutal. Beautiful.

ABOVE: 'Aren't you getting absurdly high?' Photo by Murray Close.

ANTHONY WISE
POLICEMAN 2

What did the audition entail?

Well, I tell you that very simply – I didn't audition. The casting director had actually cast an actor that I was in a theatre company with, but he couldn't do it at the last minute and they asked me if I would like to do a day's work tomorrow – it was literally like that. Bruce Robinson hadn't even seen or heard of me when I turned up on the set.

How much pressure were you under to get the motorway filming completed in a single morning?

Well, I got there about seven o'clock on Monday morning in Maida Vale made where I was told to meet, and nobody was about. People sort of rolled up you know, there was no massive sense of urgency. The other policeman's trousers were held up with safety pins at the last minute, it was that low budget.

We had to go out in full traffic on the motorway doing a few takes going round and round. I think we probably started filming about nine and the whole thing was finished by about twelve.

When I was stood there near the Westway dressed as a policeman on a corner next to the police van, a lorry pulled up and the driver said to me: 'Can you tell me the way to Kings Cross?'

I said: 'Yeah, erm, no.'

And he said: 'You're not a policeman. What are you doing dressed like that?' I'll never forget that. Even when it was filmed back in '86, the police uniform costumes we had on from the '60s must have looked well out of date.

How many takes did the arrest scene need?

I think it probably took about nine or 10. Mainly because Richard E. Grant kept corpsing when I did my line. He kept bursting out laughing, and Bruce Robinson said:

'Can you take it down a bit Anthony?' But I think he liked what I was doing. So I must have been even more hysterical in the earlier takes than I appeared in the actual film. The other policeman had no idea I was going to do the line like that. He looked at me like: 'What the hell's he saying it like *that* for?' Anyway, it's gone down in history.

What was the atmosphere like within the crew that morning?

It was great. I didn't know really what I was supposed to be doing. I'd only heard about it the day before. They sent me a script, and I still have that original *Withnail* script in my possession. I remember Paul McGann sitting there in the back of the car drunk, method acting, but I had no idea at the time what the while film was about – it was just a day's job.

How did you arrive at that manic level for 'Get in the back of the van?'

Well, because I think some policeman – when they spy a victim, driving along the road, they're looking at you and they think: 'I'm gonna get you, you little toe rag. You little spoiled brat, drinking on the motorway. *Right*. I'm going to really show you. You're just a little shit.' You know, how some police have an attitude like that, when they're in a position of authority and they come across someone that's drunk or stoned. I just did it on the spot really. I saw what the line was, and Bruce Robinson told me to go for it, so I went for it.

Were there any risky moments with that motorway filming?

Well, yes, because it was on the M40 at 9 o'clock in the morning.

We had to keep going around the roundabout to reshoot it covering the same stretch of motorway. It was quite difficult, because although they had some extra cars around us from the '60s era, obviously if any modern cars went by then it would ruin the shot, but they certainly didn't shut the motorway or anything like that. There had to be an element of pot luck.

It was 'good cop bad cop' with Robert Oates, and your timing as scene partners was perfect. How quickly did you get on the same wavelength?

Thirty seconds after 'action – go'.

Did you get a chance to socialise with the other cast that day?

No, I was back home by three o'clock in the afternoon, and had forgotten about until I saw adverts saying the film was coming up, and I thought: 'Oh, my God, this is the film I'm in.' And then in the film trailer they put my scene in. Friends of mine in America (where it was released earlier) called me and said: 'Oh, my God, Tony, we've seen you in this great movie called *Withnail & I* and God – the moment you did your bit the audience really lost it.'

It's on so many times now, it's become cult. It reminds everybody of that time when they've finished being a student, maybe with a bit of marijuana thinking: 'Yeah, I mean, I don't give a flying fuck – let's have another joint.' And then there's that horrible realisation that student life has come to an end and you actually have to get a job. It's that rite of passage transition that every student goes through. That why they relate to it, because it takes them back nostalgically to that time of their lives when they are young and free, and then reality hits. Every generation harks back to that time of their lives.

Did you get to any subsequent screenings?

I went to the showing in Leicester Square in 2000 that Richard E. Grant put on in support of his school in Swaziland, which was set up as a response to the apartheid regime. And Richard always wanted to repay his school and so he put on this show. It was my red carpet moment. I remember David and Victoria Beckham were there and they'd only just got married are were the big new thing, and people were bidding on all the props

and costumes. People were crowding the stage wanting my autograph, and then half an hour later I was out the building and no one knew who the hell I was. Complete anonymity, which was rather reassuring.

Has anyone ever shouted 'Get in the back of the van' at you?

Once they know that it's me they often do or ask me to say it. I must have been asked three or four hundred times at least. But I don't ever it off the cuff for people – that would be so boring.

I'm going to do it as a one-off for an Australian guy who wrote to me last year. A friend of his, who's in a tribute band called 'Iffy Pop', is a huge fan of *Withnail* and wanted to hear the line from me on a video for his sixtieth birthday. I'm going to do that.

What was it like working with Bruce Robinson?

Oh, he was great. I only met him for about five hours. He just seemed like a laid back dude. I was thinking: 'Oh, God, what am I doing?' Bruce said: 'Be really hostile and really, really go for it.'

Bruce did put me in one scene in his next film *How to Get Ahead in Advertising* in a bar scene. But they ended up cutting it, which was disappointing. He said he liked me that much he'd give me something in his next film.

I never got any repeat fees, it was just a low-budget movie, and nobody expected it to sort of catapult to the stage it's now at.

It's that very clever combination of getting stoned, nostalgia for days gone by, and also being very witty and funny. That's a pretty unique combination.

I'm astounded that people keep mentioning it to me over 30 years on.

I think I've only watched it twice in my life, and the second time I really, really enjoyed it. It's superbly done when you consider the budget.

IAIN MORRIS
SCREENWRITER AND DIRECTOR

Damon and I wrote the first *The Inbetweeners* movie in a small, bare, white room in Shoreditch. There were security bars on the windows, which I presume were to keep people out rather than to keep us in, but if a burglar *had* gained entry the only things kept in the office were pens, Post-it notes, and a copy of the *Withnail & I* script.

It sat there on the desk between us, acting as both inspiration and as a reminder of an unachievably high watermark in British comedy filmmaking. Occasionally, one or the other of us would pick it up, randomly flick to a page, chuckle, ruefully shake our head, and then start a discussion about how was it possible for every page to not only be funny but also say something profound about humans and their relationships with each other?

We tried to get a homage to *Withnail* in every season of *The Inbetweeners*, but every time we used a line from it, it stood out because the writing was too precise and basically too good. Someone once described the film to me as being about the difference between those who write and those who talk about writing, Marwood being the doer and Withnail the eloquent talker. All I know is that I wish I could write like that about the beauty and frustration of life.

Withnail & I is a rare film in that you can see what it's doing, but it affects you viscerally regardless. All its constituent parts – the writing, the directing, the music, the performances – are phenomenal, but it is still somehow more than the sum of those parts.

To start with the writing, the film is essentially one hilarious sketch after another, most of which, if they were to stand alone, would be among the funniest sketches you had ever seen. Even the best sketch shows tend to be a bit up and down, but in *Withnail & I* these moments work together to tell the story of the characters so beautifully. This works as an inspiration for my own writing and pushes me to try to write scenes that are as funny as sketches but feel as real and at home in the rest of the script as the best drama. I'm still working on it.

The economy of language in the film is also inspirational. That so few words are used to allow us to know the characters and their concerns is shockingly brilliant at times, passing as it does almost unnoticed.

The opening scene where Marwood repeats Withnail's 'Why can't I get a cigar commercial' is a perfect example. We know Marwood and Withnail are close because Marwood repeats the line before Withnail has finished it. He's clearly heard this a hundred times recently because he knows 'Why can't I get' – which could be followed by anything – is only ever followed by 'a cigar commercial'. Marwood knows Withnail inside out and knows he's desperate. And if Withnail is desperate then, by association, his flatmate is desperate too. With one comedic sentence, the unhappy state and weary friendship of our leading characters is revealed.

The writing of the film is often overshadowed by what must be two of the best debut film performances of all time. There's not a bad performance in the film but, for me, Richard E. Grant stands out. As a realistic portrayal of the over-confidence of the British upper classes, it's unsurpassed, but there's so much more to it. Insecurity, cowardice ('I have a heart condition') bravado ('What fucker said that?') and finally sadness and beauty.

Although he has some of the best lines in the film, Paul McGann carries us through the film with a voiceover full of a tenderness towards his friend that makes the ending even more heartbreaking.

From the supporting cast obviously Uncle Monty and Danny are marvellous, but I always particularly enjoy Michael Elphick's poacher. It remains a masterclass in 'non-stereotypical terrifying country type' and serves the sense of Withnail and Marwood being somewhere alien to them, yet *them* being the aliens, perfectly. That we see the humanity in the man who is meant to be a threat to them and, then, arguably even see

Withnail and Marwood through his eyes is testament to the brilliance of his performance.

I think the score, by (Lord) David Dundas and Rick Wentworth, is much overlooked. It's very hard to combine the melancholic and the comedic without sounding like you are laying it on too thick, or trying too hard, but the carnival-esque score lightly floats and lends both a hope and a sadness to the film with its rising major notes and falling minor ones. I also think it perfectly fits with the intention that Bruce Robinson had of the film being about the sixties ending before the decade was out, and the hangover starting early.

In terms of favourite scenes, it changes every time I watch the film; the ebb and flow of beloved scenes becomes the joy of favourite moments: Withnail slightly catching himself before saying 'acquaintance', or 'I'm in a park and I'm practically dead', or Withnail slightly corpsing in the tea shop. However, I find myself returning to the much quoted and classic moment from Marwood 'of course he's the fucking farmer', which so perfectly encapsulates the awful anger and frustration and closeness and love of friends, in one sopping wet shout. And that, really, is what the film is about to me. It's a piece of art about friendship – and how odd and weird and accepting friendships can be.

My favourite scene though is the last one. Sometimes I watch it on YouTube just for a good sob. It's an extraordinary ending as we learn that, despite not even getting a cigar commercial, Withnail really is a great classical actor and *should* play the Dane, but the only audiences that will ever know it are the wolves and the rain (and us).

ABOVE: 'Good ol' Jake.' Photo by Murray Close.

THE JOURNEY FROM CULT TO CLASSIC

BY MARTIN KEADY

The three stages of making a film are usually regarded as writing, production (the actual filming) and post-production, in which the editing, scoring and – if necessary – reshooting take place. However, there is a fourth stage that is often overlooked but which is equally important to the success, or otherwise, of a film, namely its viewing or reception by audiences and critics. The reception history of *Withnail & I* is particularly fascinating, because in the decades since the film was first released it has made the rare, if not unique, journey from cult to classic status.

Withnail & I experienced considerable difficulties even before it was released, as it took over a year to find a distributor. Then, when it finally made its way into cinemas, it was a relative failure, certainly in comparison with the previous film that Bruce Robinson had written, *The Killing Fields*, even if that was a big-budget Hollywood production and *Withnail & I* was a low-budget British production. In the beginning, *Withnail & I* garnered neither large audiences nor much in the way of critical acclaim, with the exception of the *Evening Standard* award for Best Screenplay, and it closed soon afterwards. Then, entirely fittingly for a film that is so much about its unforgettable dialogue and deft, almost unnoticeable, story-telling, *Withnail & I* gradually became extremely well-known and correspondingly successful almost entirely through word of mouth. After it had quickly come and gone from cinemas, seemingly an entire generation of students took to watching it on video, with the result that it eventually returned to cinemas, especially on the art-house and university circuit. Nevertheless, it was often misunderstood, as the hard-drinking British (and beyond) 'lad culture' of the 1990s virtually made *Withnail & I* its Bible or sacred text, so much so that it almost became more famous as a drinking game, whereby viewers tried and invariably failed to match the two protagonists drink for drink (with the foolhardiest souls even considering drinking a little lighter fluid), than it was as a film.

Fortunately, just at the point when it seemed that a subtle, beautiful and ultimately utterly truthful film about excess and its inherent dangers would forever be misunderstood as an ode to (or even instruction manual for) a life of hedonism, the general view of *Withnail & I*, both among viewers and critics, seemed to undergo an almost 360 degrees shift, such that it finally began to enjoy the 'classic' status that it had always deserved. It was as if the film's original audience had caught up with it at last; as they aged, so their appreciation of the film deepened, until it gradually came to be regarded as a masterpiece about age and ageing. And ultimately *Withnail & I* has become so much a part of its fans' lives, including those of the writers of this book, that it has become a kind of ur-text on how to adjust (or not) to the ravages of life.

Here, then, is the story of the unlikely 'afterlife' of *Withnail & I*, or an explanation of how a film about the desperate economic circumstances befalling two English actors at the end of the 1960s became one of the great narratives of our time, so much so that it is now rightly regarded as not just one of the greatest works of English or British cinema but of *all* cinema.

Video Saved The Cinema Star (The late 1980s and early 1990s)

The Coronavirus pandemic has only reinforced what has long been an increasing trend for people to watch films or television programmes either alone or in small groups, usually restricted to family members or flat or housemates. Of course, that is completely different to the original and utterly collective experience of watching a film in an actual cinema, surrounded by hundreds of fellow audience members, which was the only way to experience cinema (the earliest form of screen storytelling) until the arrival of television in the late 1940s and 1950s. Television began the erosion of the communal viewing experience that has continued ever since, and tragically it is possible that the Coronavirus pandemic has destroyed the communal viewing

OPPOSITE: *Withnail & I* screening at BAFTA. Design by Ralph Steadman.

experience, if not forever then perhaps for the foreseeable future.

However, histories of the collective viewing experience and its gradual decline throughout the second half of the 20th century and the start of the 21st century (up to and including the pandemic) often ignore a small but none the less vital period, namely the one from the mid-1980s onwards when films were first recorded and/or played on television, which is the short-lived 'Age of Video'. Now, only the name and concept remains, for example in the title of Amazon Prime Video, but for a short period (roughly from about 1980 to the early 2000s) watching a video with a group of friends who had specially gathered for that purpose was one of the last remaining ways in which a visual story, such as a film or television show, could truly be experienced collectively. And arguably no other film ever benefited so much from video and its unique viewing conditions as *Withnail & I*.

Like all the best films, *Withnail & I* has always lent itself to collective viewing, as it requires more than one person to parrot all the lines of the film (so many of which are exchanged in rapid-fire dialogue), perform all the characters and even play what eventually became the '*Withnail & I* drinking game'. Arguably, the first people ever to play that game were the cast and crew of the film, during the assorted premières and other special screenings afterwards. (For a long time, the running joke about *Withnail & I*, as it was about so many British films, was that the only people who had seen it on a cinema screen were those who were either in it or had worked on it.) Nevertheless, trying to keep up with the characters drink for drink soon became a bona fide trend, or craze, which anyone who first saw the film in the late 1980s and early 1990s (as I did) can attest to.

Of course, the obvious disadvantage of such collective viewing and drinking was that the latter often overwhelmed the former in popularity and importance. Many early viewers of the film/video discovered that it was almost humanly impossible to keep up with the imbibing of Withnail & I/Marwood, and that even

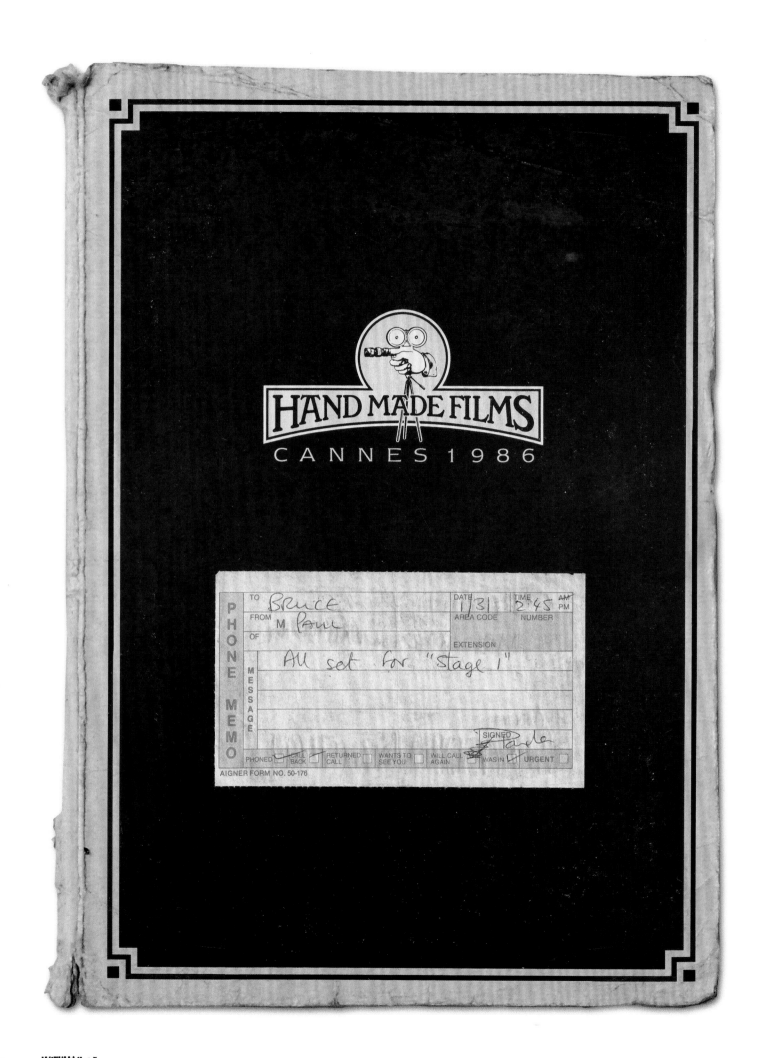

RIGHT: *Withnail & I*
Cannes film showing.

if you could, it usually meant that the actual ending of the film ended up as nothing more than a blurry haze or daze. However, the growing popularity of the film, which was further aided by its premières on various network channels (notably Britain's Channel Four, which was such a key player in the independent British cinema of the 1980s and 1990s), meant that it could finally have a viable cinematic life, as it was re-released repeatedly on the art-house and in particular the university student circuit.

Thus I was lucky enough to first experience the full glory of *Withnail & I* in the way that Bruce Robinson has always insisted is the best way to experience it – seeing it on a big screen in a cinema with full surround-sound. As a result, I could fully enjoy and appreciate both its superb dialogue and its stunning cinematography, in particular the full '15-Mile-Long Picture Postcard' effect, when I/Marwood finally emerges from Monty's house to take in the view surrounding it for the first time, which to this day remains one of the greatest cinematic 'reveals' that I have ever seen.

The return of *Withnail & I* to its rightful place in cinemas ensured that it did not become stuck in the 'video ghetto', whereby films were *only* ever watched on video, which was the fate that befell so many films in the 1980s and 1990s, including some of those made by Alex Cox, such as *Repo Man* and *Walker*. *Withnail & I* may have been reborn, or perhaps resuscitated, on video. However, anyone who truly loved the film soon came to realise that the sheer majesty of Peter Hannan's cinematography, the power of the film's score (in which the ultraviolence of Jimi Hendrix's guitar is beautifully offset by the plangent effects of David Dundas and Rick Wentworth's original score) and even the wonders of the dialogue, particularly those lines that were literally proclaimed (such as Withnail's famous 'Star!' shout-out to himself), could only be fully appreciated in cinema. Thus, the 'Age of Video', which had really begun with Buggles's eternal earworm of a pop hit, 'Video Killed The Radio Star', in 1979, finally reached its apotheosis with the same medium helping to save many films that might otherwise have been lost, or at least not seen by many people, with *Withnail & I* foremost among them.

Lads Culture and the Growing Popularity of the Drinking Game (The Rest of the 1990s)

In many ways, Britain in the 1990s was an inversion of Britain in the 1960s, and not just in the sense of simply turning a '6' upside down to create a '9'. The original and actual Sixties were a time of genuine social, economic and cultural upheaval, which is thrillingly captured in the best art made at that time (above all, the music of The Beatles) *and* the best art made about it (including *Withnail & I*, which was filmed in the 1980s but set at the end of the 1960s). By contrast, the 1990s, which had effectively begun three months early in the autumn of 1989 with its own act of genuine societal and cultural destruction and recreation (the tearing-down of the Berlin Wall, which soon led to the collapse of the entire Communist Bloc), eventually became little more than an attempt to *recreate* the 1960s, which of course completely missed the point of that uniquely inventive decade.

In music, the 'Britpop' of Blur and Oasis was heavily indebted to the original British pop and rock of the '60s, especially that of The Beatles, The Stones and The Kinks; in cinema, Anthony Minghella appeared to be making a loose sequel to David Lean's truly landmark *Lawrence of Arabia* in his screen adaptation of Michael Ondaatje's novel *The English Patient*; and even in politics, Tony Blair and Gordon Brown's repackaged (or at least renamed) 'New Labour' often seemed far less concerned with creating another 'white heat' revolution comparable to that of Harold Wilson's 1960s Labour party than it was with fending off accusations that it was still stuck in the Militant-dominated 1980s. And it was in this peculiar, at times even ersatz, context that *Withnail & I* experienced another change in how it was often viewed and received.

Having escaped 'the video ghetto', *Withnail & I* was increasingly regarded in the 1990s as the kind of classic British cinema that had barely existed at all since the short-lived Golden Age of British cinema in the 1960s. Thereafter, for much of the 1970s and 1980s British cinema was in a slump, at times appearing to consist only of uniformly awful big-screen makeovers of television sitcoms, from classics such as *Steptoe and Son* to duds

Dear Bruce,

I'm probably a sentimental old fool – and you were probably thrilled to get rid of some old stuff.

Whatever – in case Richard E. bullied you and you yielded for the sake of the lovely Africans - here's your manuscript back. I was very keen to help Richard and would have given the money anyway – and I have, I hope it's okay, taken a copy of it   (sometimes the back of pages too) because it's a gripping document, and I'm about to go away for 5 months to Bali and would love to read it lounging amongst the mosquitoes. (So far I've only read half of page 1 – and already a very, very good joke indeed).

I hope you've recovered from whatever it was that was whacking you at the screening.

Best wishes to you, and the family and your cheekily named farm.

Richard Curtis.

> **"*Withnail & I* often appeared to be the exception that proved the rule – a brilliantly written, directed and acted British film."**

(and offensive duds at that) such as *On The Buses*. Consequently, in the 1990s *Withnail & I* often appeared to be the exception that proved the rule – a brilliantly written, directed and acted British film, in a cinematic landscape where there were very few other British films of such quality, if any. It seemed that nearly a decade after Richard Griffiths had famously lamented to Bruce Robinson after the film's initial box-office failure, 'They didn't get it, Bruce', British viewers and indeed viewers around the world were finally beginning to 'get' *Withnail & I*.

At the same time, however, the film suffered from being swept up in the contemporary love of all things British (especially the truly great British culture of the 1960s) and submerged in a generally laddish and particularly heavy-drinking culture that had more in common with Hogarth's depictions of the 'gin lanes' of the 18th century than the free love, free thinking and liberal drug-taking of the 1960s. Probably the pinnacle of that distressing trend was the purchase for £5,000 of the coat that Richard E. Grant wore as Withnail by Chris Evans, the unofficial spokesman of the increasingly coarse and unsophisticated mainstream culture of the 1990s. In effect, *Withnail & I*, having escaped one ghetto (video) was now being ghettoised in an even worse way, by being reduced to little more than the 'eye-track' or prompt-book for an even more aggressive and even antagonistic version of the *Withnail & I* drinking game, one that was far more likely to end with the participants in hospital or a police station than it was to culminate in the personal and artistic enlightenment that the film was really all about.

Therefore, a decade or so after its initial release, and having survived initially being a commercial failure in cinemas to become the original 'phoenix film' that was reborn on video, *Withnail & I* now faced another tragic fate, namely being more widely watched but also often completely misunderstood.

The Acquisition of Classic Status (2000 onwards)

Fortunately for the film, its creators and its true fans, from about the year 2000 onwards – the fabled 'Millennium', which was so feverishly looked forward to and then almost immediately forgotten about afterwards – *Withnail & I* experienced another critical rehabilitation. This time, it was one that afforded it not the novelty status of a 'party game' but the genuinely classic status of a great film.

In large part, this was because the original audience for the film (those students who had first provided it with a real audience in the late 1980s and early 1990s) was ageing and maturing with it. In other words, they were undergoing precisely the kind of life and outlook change that I/Marwood experiences in the film and that Withnail himself is ultimately utterly incapable of. Ironically, the kind of 'mass falling out' of people that Danny the Dealer had envisaged at the end of the film and the end of the decade in which it is set – 'London is a city coming down from its trip and there's going to be a lot of refugees' – probably happened on a greater scale (at least in number) at the end of the 1990s/turn of the Millennium. As 'refugees' from reality of all kinds, ranging from celebrities such as Chris Evans himself to a large number of ordinary 'lads' and even 'ladettes', sought rehabilitation and detoxification after a long period of excess, *Withnail & I* was no longer solely viewed through alcohol-bleared eyes but, perhaps for the first time, viewed soberly, even maturely, by viewers and critics alike.

That critical and cultural rehabilitation has continued ever since, with far less emphasis on the main characters' drinking and far more on the film's undoubted merits. In a way, it was as if the influence of I/Marwood himself, the dutiful and relatively clear-eyed chronicler of the story, became more important, having initially been almost overwhelmed by the antics and sheer cinematic presence of his partner in crime.

It was now possible to place *Withnail & I* within a tradition that is peculiarly English but with universal resonance. It might be called sublime melancholy and it extends throughout the entirety of English story-telling, literature and cinema: from Chaucer, the supposed 'Father of English', whose *Canterbury Tales* is another ostensibly bawdy and raucous work that actually contains hidden Himalayas of meaning; through Shakespeare, particularly in the

OPPOSITE: Letter from director Richard Curtis accompanying the original *Withnail & I* manuscript Richard bought at a charity auction and returned to Bruce.

ABOVE: Bruce's script – written in 1970 – is more relevant than ever. Photo: Karl Nesh / Shutterstock.com

ample form of Falstaff and Hal; right up to the classic 20th century cinema of (British-born Stan) Laurel and Hardy, and the elegies to England and Englishness of Graham Greene and Harold Pinter, particularly Pinter's screenplay for *The Go-Between*.

In addition, the influence of *Withnail & I* on other screenwriters and film-makers became evident. There were two superb American films, *Swingers* (1996) and *Sideways* (2004), that almost reset and recast *Withnail & I* in America, as they told remarkably similar stories about struggling actors and writers trying to come to terms with apparently inevitable failure *and* the deterioration of their closest friendships. In Britain, with its far smaller film industry, the influence of *Withnail & I* was probably more profound on television programmes, particularly *Peep Show*, which arguably became Britain's greatest ever sitcom (at least in terms of scale, as its total of nine seasons was far greater than that of much shorter-lived sitcoms such as *Fawlty Towers* and *Porridge*) and its creators, Jesse Armstrong and Sam Bain, always openly acknowledged the influence of *Withnail & I* upon their work. And even the biggest British television success of the 21st century so far, *Fleabag*, Phoebe Waller-Bridge's tragicomedy about an apparently free-spirited young woman who is actually haunted by the death of her best

friend, surely owed a debt to *Withnail & I*. If the main characters were sisters rather than friends, then 'Fleabag' herself (played by Waller-Bridge) was in some ways, at least at the start, a sort of female Withnail, especially in her heavy drinking.

Of course, *Withnail & I* itself has been given new life and increased popularity by the internet and in particular social media. For example, numerous Facebook groups extol the glories of the film, recycle its lines and apply them to situations and news stories that have nothing to do with the film (once again showing not only its infinite quotability but the apparently infinite applicability of so many of its greatest lines), as well as sharing fan art and personal stories about what the film means to them. One particularly poignant example was the member of the *Withnail & I Appreciation Society* Facebook Group who declared that, having become an alcoholic himself and therefore having had to stop drinking, he viewed the film completely differently through his new-found sobriety. And if Bruce Robinson himself remains a resolute non-user of social media, Richard E. Grant often goes to the other extreme, most recently posting clips during the Pandemic in which he recited some of Withnail's most famous lines before immediately collapsing with laughter.

There has also been increasing interest in, even fascination with, Bruce Robinson himself and his other work. Having initially committed himself to film after making *Withnail & I*, making a good living as a writer-director and a couple of fairly good films in *How To Get Ahead In Advertising* (1989) and *Jennifer 8* (1992), he eventually returned to his true métier, which was writing in all its forms. He produced the two other parts of what might loosely be called 'The Bruce Robinson Trilogy': *The Peculiar Memories of Thomas Penman* (1998), which was a semi-autobiographical account of his own experience of being an unhappy post-war child ('I was brought up like sick'); and the non-fiction epic *They All Love Jack: Busting The Ripper* (2015), in which, having conducted the kind of uber-meticulous research that had become his hallmark on screenplays such as *The Killing Fields* and *Fat Man and Little Boy*, he applied his literary detective skills to the most famous unsolved criminal case of them all – who really was Jack The Ripper? Along with the script and film of *Withnail & I*, these two works effectively constitute a lifetime's (or at least a late lifetime's) work, ensuring that Robinson will hopefully not solely be remembered for *Withnail & I*.

In addition, Robinson can take comfort from the fact that *Withnail & I* is no longer solely or even largely seen as a guide to how to Drink Too Much. In several interviews, including those for Alistair Owen's *Smoking In Bed: Conversations With Bruce Robinson* (2001) and those conducted for this book, Robinson has admitted to being uncomfortable with certain aspects of the film's reception and certain elements of its audience, in particular the *reductio ad absurdum* of the drinking game. Hopefully, he can finally rest assured that most new and even most old fans of the film have come to regard it as, among many other things, a bitter-sweet evocation of the glories and dangers of drinking, which can ultimately lead, as is surely the case with Withnail himself, to alcoholism and all its attendant misery.

What Next? (or The Future for *Withnail & I*)

So, what next for *Withnail & I*? In the first instance, it is arguably one of the most important films – indeed, one of the most important works of art – for viewing Britain in its new-found position post-Brexit. As a devotee of Baudelaire and Huysmans, it is extremely unlikely that Bruce Robinson would have any truck with Brextremists. Nevertheless, like all the very greatest works of art, the aesthetics of *Withnail & I* are ultimately infinitely more important than its politics, or, as Uncle Monty famously and even-handedly put it: 'Shat on by Tories, shovelled up by Labour'.

It will also be absolutely fascinating to see how *Withnail & I* fares in what might be called 'the post-Woke world'. The remarkably loosely defined (if it is properly defined at all) 'Woke' movement, in which the majority of people in Western society are increasingly aware of the iniquities and inequities faced by many of its minorities, especially those of a different skin colour to the majority, has savaged many works of art for their explicit or even implicit racism, sexism and homophobia. It will certainly be instructive to see whether *Withnail & I*, with its references to 'Queers', 'Micks' and 'Spades' (not to mention the almost entire absence of women), can survive being 'cancelled' by the increasingly militant mainstream culture.

However, the likelihood is that having already seen off so much opposition, from the early indifference of distributors and critics to the occasional caricaturing of it as just a silly cult film about drinking, *Withnail & I* will ultimately proclaim, to those who are supposedly 'Woke' but in reality often remain prejudiced themselves, the ultimate Withnailian put-down: 'You can stuff it up your arse for nothing and fuck off while you're doing it'.

All of that, if it is to happen at all, is for the future. For now, *Withnail & I* and its creator, Bruce Robinson, can rest assured that it has already attained the only immortality that any of us can ever enjoy – the artistic kind – as there can be no doubt that when the definitive history of late 20th century/early 21st century Britain and the art it produced in all media finally comes to be written, *Withnail & I* will be at the very least a substantial footnote and quite conceivably even a chapter all on its own. That is because in the 35 years since it was filmed and released, it has become arguably the most brilliant and certainly the most beloved – indeed, *adored* – of all British films.

JOURNALIST

At its heart, *Withnail & I* is a road movie and their infamous car, a MkII Jaguar in a wretched state of disrepair, steals every scene it appears in. Missing a headlamp and pocked with rust, the scabrous vehicle is despair on wheels.

'It looked pretty horrible!' says the film's art director Henry Harris. 'But it was an extension of their life. It had to sit with their flat. It couldn't stand apart from what was happening in there.'

By the end of the Sixties, a well-used MkII was cheap and, thanks to its popularity as a bank robbers' getaway car, had acquired a rather rakish image. It was the perfect ride for a pair of desperate Thespians with grand dreams and empty pockets. Like everything in their world, their car is falling apart around them. Yet it has a certain distressed style. Reduced to the status of a wreck it may be, but it's still a Jag. In their minds they're not poor, just broke.

Along with Bruce Robinson and production designer Michael Pickwoad, art director Henry helped create the iconic *Withnail* Jaguar. They sourced the prop car through a movie vehicle specialist called John Geary and the first one he showed them got the part: a pale grey 1961 example with a six-cylinder, 2.4 litre XK engine (the same motor as Inspector Morse's famous MkII) with the registration number 405SBH.

'The colour was really good, that dull grey. We didn't want anything bright metallic or red or anything like that. It had to be dreary,' says Henry.

The only drawback was the condition of the bodywork: it was too good. So to achieve full *Withnail* banger spec, the props crew painted on rust, pulled off various chrome bits, removed both rear wheel arches, plucked out a headlamp and binned one windscreen wiper. The result was so convincingly decrepit you can almost smell the musty aroma of mouldy carpet, rotting leather, leaking petrol and spilled claret.

The Jaguar was an autobiographical choice, too. 'Bruce had a similar car in the late Sixties and he was keen to get one,' says Henry. Back then Robinson's actress girlfriend Lesley-Anne Down bought him 'a fucked old Jag'. But it was neither as old or as fucked as the *Withnail* car, which already had 25 years on the clock by the time it arrived on set.

During his struggling actor years, Bruce took his own battered MkII to the Lake District, accompanied by his actor friend Michael Feast; an ill-fated road trip which inspired Withnail and Marwood's dismal rural odyssey. But unlike their Jag, Bruce's didn't make it home. Instead he drove it into a ditch, whereupon a farmer (who really was called Parkin) came along, hooked it up his tractor and ripped off the entire front of the car. 'It wasn't funny at the time,' said Robinson ruefully when I interviewed him for the film's 20th anniversary in 2007.

Henry Harris also discovered the over-the-top Rolls-Royce limousine driven by Uncle Monty.

'I'd just bought a copy of 'Car and Classic' and was looking through it, and Michael (Pickwoad) the designer said 'We've got to get a really silly car for Uncle Monty' and I showed him this thing that was up for sale,' he said,

It was a 1953 Silver Wraith Sedanca de Ville limousine, custom-made by notable coach-builder Hooper & Co for Nubar Gulbenkian, an Armenian oil magnate who was then one of the world's richest men.

'So I said to John Geary, 'Do you think there's any chance we can get it?' And we did! We got it for a day, but it cost quite a lot of money. It was quite steep for our budget but it was worth it.'

With its snakeskin-trimmed doors and dash and speedometer in the rear to check the chauffeur was making time, it was tailor-made for a flamboyant upper-class eccentric. 'It was a ridiculous thing.' says Henry Harris. 'Suited Uncle Monty perfectly.'

The scene where Hendrix's guitar wails, the wrecking ball swings, Marwood flips down his shades and lurches away in the rotten Jag is one of the film's most memorable moments. It was filmed early one Sunday morning on Freston Road, north of Shepherd's Bush in North West London. And if you look carefully, you can spot Bruce Robinson's own silver 1962 Aston Martin DB4 Convertible parked on the right as they drive away.

'The set people were saying 'We've got to move those effing cars', but I said it's all right, it's in period. No problem. So it stayed there,' explained Bruce, whose fascination with Astons began as an eight-year-old schoolboy, thanks to a family friend called Johnny Withnall (Bruce purloined the name but changed the spelling).

An incorrigible rogue, Withnall drove a DB2 which he once reversed out of a pub car park straight into the side of a police car. Obliterated on booze, he once took the young Bruce out for a spin, stopping occasionally to fling open the door and spew into the gutter. Bruce was thrilled: 'He was the coolest guy I'd ever met in my life. He used to drive in a state of complete Messerschmitt pilot danger. Completely pissed. And I really fancied all of that when I was a kid. That turned me on to Astons.'

In 1981, Bruce finally found the car of his boyhood dreams up on blocks in a Fulham garage where it had sat for eighteen years with under 30,000 miles on the odometer. A rare drophead DB4, it was one of just seventy Aston Martin produced between 1961 and 1963.

'Even though it was falling to bits it cost me eight grand, a lot of money then, and I spent another fifteen grand getting it back on the road,' said Bruce, who would go on to spend well in excess of £100,000 restoring and upgrading the car over the years, installing a 4.0-litre Vantage engine and modified final drive for extra 'oomph'.

'The weird thing about the standard DB4 is that it was actually underpowered,' he said back in 2007. 'My one is considerably heated up. It's got a low-ratio back end and it whacks through the gears much, much faster. It will supposedly hit 150 miles an hour but who wants that? I'd rather have it go like a rocket up to a hundred. After that it's appearances in court anyway, isn't it?'

Despite its value and rarity, Bruce used the Aston as a daily driver, for tooling around London and long haul trips to his South of France holiday home. 'I just love the shape and the design and for years and years I never bothered with anything else, really.' It also starred in his *Withnail* follow-up *How To Get Ahead In Advertising*.

After 28 years of ownership, Bruce sold his beloved Aston in 2009 for £241,000. 'It has become like an Old Master now and it moves you into an arena you don't want to be in – you know, flash gits,' he explained. 'Besides which I live on a farm down a long muddy track. It seems heartless to get it caked in duck shit and up to its axles in mud.

'Anyway all the things I used to love about driving – like drinking and going fast – are illegal nowadays,' he lamented. 'I used to race about in the Aston up to my shoulders in empties. You can't do anything like that any more, can you?'

ABOVE: Jag Mk 2 405 SBH fitted with rain rig.

MATTHEW BINNS
UNIT PRODUCTION MANAGER

Can you tell us about your location scouting for *Withnail*?

I started on the film in May '86. I read the script before I met Bruce, and I loved it. Because I lived with my girlfriend next to Camden in Primrose Hill and was going through a life crisis having recently realized I wasn't a teenager anymore, the script resonated with me. Plus the fact that I had spent most of my time in London walking around in Camden Town and Notting Hill and the Golborne road and All Saints Road area. I didn't grow up in England, I grew up in Malta and Jamaica, so I was getting to know London in the exact area where the film was set. So I could imagine the film's locations and had an idea what Bruce was looking for.

I also knew the Lake District because I had inherited some land on the edge of Lake Coniston, so I'd been up there a few times, and had a handle on that area. My first thoughts were obviously Crow Crag because we were going to start shooting on location (as one always does) at the beginning of the schedule, to get what's seen as the most challenging and most expensive part of the film out of the way- because you've got your crew on location.

I'd had several meetings with Bruce and Paul Heller at a house that Paul had rented in Peel Street, Holland Park, just south of Notting Hill Gate. We had a few drinks at The Churchill, just round the corner. That's where I met Bruce and Paul. They were in the midst of casting with Mary Selway, so there were actors coming and going the whole time. I remember bumping into Michael Elphick there at one point and Richard E. Grant at another.

For a month, I was on the search for an abandoned farmhouse. The more Southern parts of the Lake District that I knew were closer to the cities and there was more development – it was a bit more gentrified, whereas if you carried on up to North Cumbria it became more rural. I love looking at maps, and have found locations on a lot of movies over the years. It's

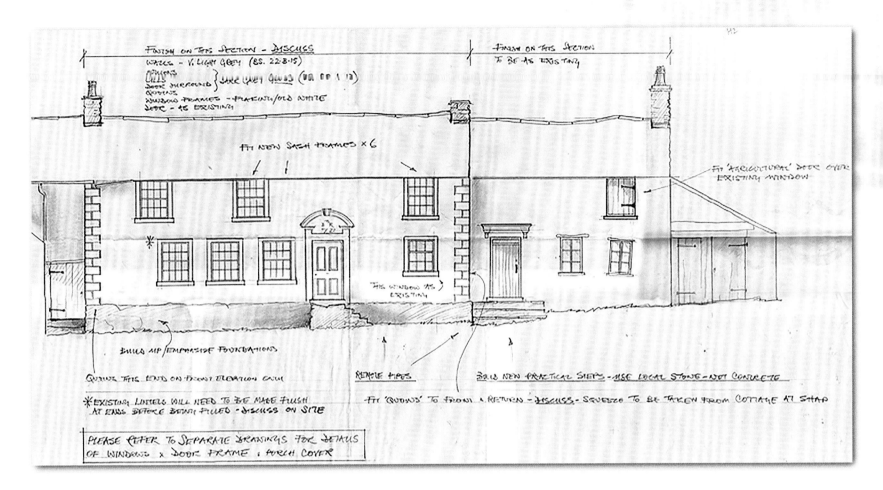

such fun to look at a map and figure it out, just to see what might be there. One didn't yet have the internet, so I was using Ordnance Survey maps, the one inch to the mile variety, and a lot of legwork.

I drove down this road and followed the map, and even though there were gates, I kept on pushing on, past another farmhouse then took a left turn, and ended up coming down a track, and the setting of Sleddale Hall appeared as you approached it, and you got this great view of this courtyard of the house. And it just seemed to lend itself to Bruce's vision – some faded architectural details of what must once have some grandeur, but abandoned in the wildness.

We'd looked at a couple of other places, and I'd go back to London, with lots of photographs, and I'd make presentations. But you get a feeling when a place seems to be right.

After I'd found Crow Crag, I met them off the train, and we went to the hotel called The George in Penrith. It's like a classic old three-star pub hotel. The next morning, we went off to look at three farmhouses. But you could see on Bruce and Paul's faces when we came up to Crow Crag – that reaction when they first saw this incredible location.

Bruce and I were walking along this little path, by the house down towards this lake I wanted to show them. There's a reservoir right next to Sleddale Hall, which is why it was owned by Northwest water. Paul was doing this sort of thing you do when you make a camera shot using your hands. He was walking backwards doing a tracking shot of us, and getting excited probably imagining some scene where Bruce is Withnail & I'm Marwood or something, all the time walking backwards, the farmhouse in the background. But Paul couldn't see what I could see, which was a cliff he was about to tumble over. I ran ten feet towards him and did a rugger tackle just before he went over the edge. Bruce fell about laughing of course.

When you're figuring out the jigsaw puzzle of where the scenes take place, it's just a tiny part of it all. Because, of course, the actors and all the other elements that bring a film together -the makeup and the wardrobe and props, filming, light and sound and so many other elements need considering – but getting the location right like this was such a crucial starting point, and there's just something about Sleddale Hall. Michael Pickwoad came along three weeks later and had about three or four weeks of prep to create the look he and Bruce wanted for Monty's cottage.

David Wimbury and I had done six films together at that point, and we were a bit of a production team. It wasn't always automatic, because you might be off doing something else when a film gets

OPPOSITE: Bruce heads North.

ABOVE: Michael Pickwoad sketch of Crow Crag. Michael Pickwoad passed away 27th of August 2017.

green-lit. It's why I didn't end up working on *How to Get Ahead in Advertising*, because I was in Jamaica production-managing *The Mighty Quinn*, one of Denzel Washington's early films.

I put Bruce and Paul back on the train to London, and they were happy campers. It tells you a bit about David Wimbury, because he was travelling up on the train and arrived at the station about 10 minutes after Bruce and Paul had left. He was allowing Bruce and Paul to have that location discovery without him being around – to leave them to their process. He would have orchestrated it that way.

David arrived and we went to Sleddale Hall and I 'downloaded' what they had liked – what scenes, what would work where – that kind of thing. And so we decided – based on what they wanted to do – how we would make that work. We worked out at that point that given the whole seven weeks really wasn't very long, it was going to be just over two weeks at Sleddale Hall. That was a key thing, so we decided that for practical reasons at this location, we didn't have the money for make-up trailers, wardrobe, buses, and all that kind of stuff that you'd have on location in London. So our first plan was to do what you customarily do on low budget films – you try to rent a house next door – but there wasn't one because it was a remote farm. So we used the upstairs, but that was even more dilapidated – the roof wasn't that great, so we had to do a lot of repairs to turn that into make-up, hair, wardrobe and dressing rooms for the boys. None of the scenes set upstairs at Crow Crag were actually shot at Sleddale Hall. We rented a farmhouse that we would always rent very close to Shepperton studios, called Stockers Farm, which is a sort of to go-to farmhouse for the film industry. The art department just dressed to match, because the viewer has never seen the upstairs – so as long as the windows matched, that was all that really mattered.

There are some scenes where someone rushes upstairs or there's Uncle Monty rushing downstairs, and all of that, we would work that all out where that would need to be shot. Production likes to keep the creative juices flowing, keep everybody happy, but at the same time figure out how to do it efficiently.

OPPOSITE: Sleddale Hall. Photograph by Pete Savin.

HANDMADE FILMS (PRODUCTIONS) LTD

EXTENDED DAY

PRODUCTION: "WITHNAIL & I"   CALL SHEET NO: 7

DIRECTOR: BRUCE ROBINSON   DATE: Monday 21 July 1986

LOCATION: A. Sleddale Hall   UNIT CALL:
                Wet Sleddale   Leave hotel: 08:00
                Nr. Shap   On location: 08:30

            B. Public Telephone Booth
                Bampton

            C. Ash Hill
                Rosgill
                Nr. Bampton

            D. Rose Cottage
                Rosgill
                Nr. Bampton
            (See Movement Order No.3)

SETS:		SCENE NOS:
A:	1. INT. COTTAGE LIVING ROOM	1. 61, 76, 108 DAY
	INT. COTTAGE LIVING ROOM	64 pt. to comp. NIGHT
	2. INT. COTTAGE P.O.V.	2. 49 pt. DAY
	3. EXT. HILL OVER COTTAGE	3. 55 DAY
B:	4. EXT. COUNTRYSIDE & PHONE BOOTH	4. 69, 70 DAY
C:	5. INT. JAG	5. 42 NIGHT
D: S/BY:	6. EXT. LAKESIDE ROAD	6. 73 NIGHT

ACTOR	CHARACTER	P/UP	M/UP & W/be	ON SET
Richard Grant	Withnail	07:30	08:00	09:00
Paul McGann	Marwood	07:30	08:00	09:00
CROWD				
Sean Newson				08:30
Jeremy Cargill				08:30

ART DEPT/PROPS   as per script to include: "Draft Deflector", boiling
                water, carrier bags & string, loaves, stew, cold lamb,
                hot potatoes, Monty's note, telegram, telephone booth,
                two shilling piece, grocery bag, Jaguar, whiskey, map.

SFX   Wind, smoke, fire in grate, rain on windows. Car to be
        rigged as far as possible during a.m.

CAMERA/SOUND   Rushes must be wrapped at lunchtime &
                leave location by 14.00.
                Car to be rigged as far as possible during a.m.

M/UP/HAIR   Actors to be made up at cottage.

WARDROBE   Actors to be dressed at cottage.

PRODUCTION   Breakfast in hotels available from 07:00. Call sheets
                will be available daily in reception at each hotel.
                Car Rig & A-Frame (Scene 42), Cherry Picker (Scene 55).

RUSHES VIEWING   North Lakes Hotel as advised.

Contd.

THIS PAGE: Call sheet including the Bampton phone box scene. 'Well lick ten percent of the arses for me. Hello? Hello? Hello? Hello? How dare you! Fuck you.'

What do you feel were Paul Heller's most crucial moments in helping make *Withnail* the ultimate success it's become?

Well, I think Paul's most crucial influence is that the film would never have happened without him. Paul saw the script and he loved it. He had this eye for something quirky – something special. Producers generally search for certain things in a script, such as: are these roles suitable for stars? How easy is it going to be to cast this film? We all get sucked into a sort of formula for making a successful film. But those criteria don't lend themselves to the most original movies.

Specifically with this film, Paul told Bruce that he should direct it. Because Bruce was so specific about what he wanted, and how he wanted the lines in his script delivered. Paul's concern was it might never get made otherwise, because Paul might never find a director who would do exactly what Bruce wanted, so he convinced Bruce to direct it. Bruce didn't think Paul would be able to get the money with him directing, which was a fair enough assessment at that time, but Paul did. HandMade put up a chunk of the money and Paul also brought some money independently.

How long did you get in Monty's townhouse in Glebe Place, and what are your memories of shooting there?

It was Bernard Neville's house. He was a creative director. An absolutely amazing location, right down there on the river. Bernard had this incredible studio that he'd turned into a library. He collected quite a lot of amazing stuff. All the paintings and incredible furniture were there already. We had very limited time – a day to get it all done. The art department weren't allowed to mess with anything that was there already. We had to control how many members of the crew could actually go in and limit it to X number of people. Of course we had to do that anyway because of that dastardly cat!

How nervous were HandMade on that first visit to Sleddale Hall?

HandMade were certainly nervous and risk-averse. Guys like Denis O'Brien were all terrified of the financial disaster that had

happened a few years previously on the film, *Heaven's Gate*, and again when problems on the Al Pacino starrer *Revolution* had just caused the collapse of Goldcrest. Accounts types, like – Denis O'Brien, were concerned that something like that would happen to them on *Withnail*. Given how small our budget was compared to a blockbuster failing it all seemed a bit disproportionate.

I remember from the first day, when Dennis totally freaked out. What we planned for the first day shooting up at Crow Crag was to make *the actors* comfortable right from the start. We were shooting inside, it was all dark, and Withnail and Marwood had to find oil lamps, and they were wandering around with candles. We were shooting in sequence – what a director wants to do is try and keep in sequence as much as possible. Given that we started our schedule at the farmhouse, shooting the interior arrival

ABOVE: 'I think we've been in here too long.' Chepstow Place W2.

ABOVE: Associate producer Lawrence Kirstein, producer Paul Heller with Bruce on an early scout of Wet Sleddale Reservoir.

scenes first that morning with the farmhouse draped in blackout made perfect sense.

But actually, what a lot of producers often do is to give the money people some candy – you've got to give them some money shots and instant gratification to calm them down: 'We're making a movie – look at our first action scene – it's incredible.'

Instead, they got these dark, desperate first scenes, and they totally, totally freaked out. Bruce quit, and there was a bit of a kerfuffle – all on the first day. David sorted them all out, of course. David had the relationship with HandMade, having done three films with them, and knew how to get everybody back on track – what to ignore, and what not to ignore, and all of that. The politics of the whole thing. David knew how to handle all of that stuff.

Did you get involved in The Mother Black Cap shoot?

Michael Pickwoad found that location. I knew the place perfectly well; it was called The Tavistock Arms back then – a pretty rundown old pub. I immediately knew it when Pickwoad told me about it. When you find a location, the first thing you need to do is check out the feasibility of actually shooting it. So I went and saw the owners – did a deal with them, got a location release, and showed evidence of insurance. The art department would have needed a few hours, and then we shot it that day, it was one of a number of London locations we were working on.

Any memories of creating the Penrith Tea Rooms set?

David [Wimbury], Peter Kohn (the Assistant Director) and I would go through this process of looking at all the locations in the film, and decide which ones we absolutely had to keep on location in the Lake District. And we ended up coming up with Crow Crag, the farmer's house with the tractor, and there's a few odd little ones, that don't matter where they are shot but better with the Cumbria backdrop, like the phone box, we ended up shooting that near Sleddale. We always knew it would be silly to to keep a whole crew on location when we're not really featuring Penrith. It was never really in the script. So the tea rooms were shot near Milton Keynes, and we combined it with the pub. The art department had to go in and fiddle around with it. I think it was an estate agents that was fairly easy to convert over with a few tables and chairs and stuff.

How did you find the jag and other vintage cars and vans and tractor?

That was really an extension of the art department. On a bigger film, you'd have a guy to source and deliver the vehicles to set. Michael Pickwoad would have looked after this. I think my mate Ian helped. He had supplied all the cars for *The Long Good Friday*. I knew all about Mark II Jags, I was really fond of them. My mother had one when I was growing up in Malta. The funny thing was I was walking down the street in Penrith while the film was shooting in Cumbria, and what sails by but a *beautiful*, absolutely perfect black Mark II Jag. It's nothing like the one on the film, which we had to drive around on a trailer, because it would break down all the time – dreadful. And we didn't have the money to have a proper mechanic every day the cars worked. Usually on a film, you'll have a dedicated Picture Car department looking after all the vehicles.

But this black jag was the most beautiful car I'd ever seen, and I ran down the street when he pulled up – a sweet little guy who'd retired and spent the past two years rebuilding this from a shell – all from new parts. He had an E-type jag in the garage as well, and really wanted to move on to that, so he'd decided that morning he would sell it for £2,400, so I bought it on the spot right there in Penrith and kept it until 2003.

> **"For somebody who was making his first film, he really did know what he wanted in terms of performance. And that's such a powerful thing – the crew could see something special was going on."**

How did Bruce Robinson's directing approach differ from the other directors you'd worked with at that time?

Well he was an actor, which is key, and the fact that he wrote it, and was obsessed with the actors getting it right. In those days, what everybody was talking about was doing a bit of improvisation – entire movies of improv. But Bruce was the antithesis of improvisation, and that's where it's tricky because you could get bogged down in trying to get perfection, which probably happened a couple of times. But generally what Bruce got was what led the film to being such an amazing piece, because he had the movie inside his head, and he just did the best to get that out there.

There are other directors out there who believe their actors are geniuses at what they do, and they want to leave it to them to empower them to their best work, and end up relinquishing much process to them. Bruce, in a funny way (because his world was so much within the actor's world) let them do their thing for sure, but it was a very collaborative process. For somebody who was making his first film, he really did know what he wanted in terms of performance. And that's such a powerful thing – the crew could see something special was going on.

The other key thing that people don't often realise is that we'd all worked together before. A big chunk of us had done lots of films together, including Peter Hannan, the cinematographer, and Bob Smith. I'd done five or six movies with Bob Smith, so I knew that he was one of the best camera operators – which is not surprising, given that Peter Hannan was one of the best cinematographers you could ever get. To have somebody like Bob Smith when you're making your first film was a huge help for Bruce.

Bruce knew exactly what he wanted, without being a technician. He wanted the story told from McGann's point of view, so Marwood was watching, but he didn't want to get bogged down in that either. So, once Bruce explained what he wanted, Peter and Bob were just geniuses at giving him that. It's not a movie that's full of 'over the shoulder' shots, which lesser people would have done. *Oh, we're making it from Marwood's point of view, so we'll have all the shots with Marwood's shoulder.* It's not that. I recall the

scenes that took place in uncle Monty's, for example. There were two sofas, and the way Bruce originally plotted the scene out, we would have probably not gotten out of that wonderful location in the time allowed. But Bob had a quiet word in Bruce's ear, and said that if we shot it it this way, we can actually light the whole scene from one side, and shoot it much quicker because we don't have to keep on changing the lighting setup. So that's the thing, you've got a great camera team helping the director consider what's more valuable. Is it to have all the time you want with your actors and not have to worry about waiting for Lighting, or have actors sitting where you might have preferred, but end maybe shoot yourself in the foot? So when you've got experienced people around you, you get saved. There are always compromises but you need good advice. It's like doing something in your house and hiring a really, really good contractor who's not just there to rip you off but makes you feel happy that you get the most out of the work. So these guys just did an incredible job. And, Peter Hannan – everybody knows him. He's done some amazing films.

People don't really understand the relationship the camera operator has with a director. These were in the days before you had video assist. Nowadays, people don't even think about it because they're watching what the camera operator's watching on a monitor, in a tent outside the set. But in those days, it was still long enough ago that it was the old school – shooting on film, and you don't want to keep on using up film unnecessarily. So you need to have a very efficient way of getting what you want, and if the director can't be looking through the camera, then you need somebody who *completely* knows what the director wants, and can tell him that was it. Because the next time the director sees it is next day when the film is being processed, and you're seeing yesterday's footage in dailies for the first time and you're no longer, say, filming at Uncle Monty's. The operator was *so* key, and Bob's contribution to the film was vital.

You hire your director of photography and then the operator and then they hire the lighting guys. So we had the same lighting and camera guys we knew from other films we'd worked on. We

ABOVE: Sleddale Hall as it was in 2011 (left) and in 2013 (right), after Tim Ellis completed the restoration.

always ended up hiring Peter Frampton and Sue Love on makeup and hair, if they were available. So in fact, we were a little family really. The makeup department, wardrobe, everybody, really. The only people that in my day I didn't really interact that much with were the editing department. He'd be going through each day's shoot, and assembling dailies, and sequences. So sometimes there'd be an editor up on location. But once we got back to Shepperton, you could walk over to the cutting rooms and chat. One of the assistant editors was a friend – Anne Sopel, so I'd go over and see it, but that was a different part of the process, one that I know Bruce got into very deeply. Paul Heller was there, that's the whole point of the producer. He's the guy who said Bruce should direct it, and then he was there to lend support to Bruce when the film was being cut.

How did Paul Heller and David Wimbury's roles differ?

Paul was the guy who was protecting the creative. Part of his job was to help Bruce. He was basically investing in his career, because he's saying: 'You can do this, and I'm going to help you along the way.' Paul was a creative. But to be a creative to that degree, and have the respect of money, you have to have a track record. And Paul had been a studio exec at Warner Brothers, and he'd made films that were tiny budgets as well that had become huge. I'd recently been working with him on a sequel to *Enter the Dragon* which he was one of the original producers of, and that was pretty huge compared to the original movie – a completely different world of filmmaking. He had the respect of all kinds of executives because he'd been one. But at the same time, he

was a supporter of the creatives and always was a champion of diversity and emerging talent.

David's role was really a sort of managing director, so his clients in a way were HandMade – who were bankrolling most of the film. And so his allegiance would be to HandMade because, after all, we'd made lots of films with them. So if a decision had to be made, and it affected our relationship with HandMade, he might end up being the advocate for that HandMade point of view. David was a genius at keeping everything balanced, between keeping HandMade at bay, but at the same time being happy enough to remain at bay, and let us get on with making the film. But still very much administering the film. Valerie ran his office and was the production coordinator, so she and I were very close. We worked together on all the agreements that I was handling. I didn't handle the talent agreements, as David was handling those. Paul didn't have to get tied up in the admin, as David, Valerie and I would take care of all that.

You're not meant to tie the director up in anything other than concentrating on the script and the film and what they need. Basically, the whole point of production is to service the director and the camera. And that's the point of every department really, be it the makeup artist or the camera department. You have to channel communications so not everybody's going up to the director and asking questions. You have to fight confusion. It's a bit of a military ethos in filmmaking. You have to have a sort of a chain of command as to who it is who has access to the director, so heads of departments do, so people that work for them go to their department head – it's just the natural hierarchy.

TIM ELLIS
CURRENT OWNER OF SLEDDALE HALL

What made you decide to buy Sleddale Hall?

I suppose ultimately it was fate. A neighbour when I was living in Canterbury was a big fan of the film and had visited the house in the Lake District and told me it was derelict. I thought it would have been someone's pride and joy. I wrote to United Utilities in 2006 asking if they owned it, and if they'd like to sell it. They wrote back and said yes they did and no they wouldn't.

The house came up for auction in 2009 in a blitz of media publicity, and the night before I thought: 'What the hell' and went to London and ended up being the under-bidder. When the winning bid fell through I got a call from the auctioneers asking if I was still interested, and obviously the answer was yes.

Was there anything that was familiar from the film when you walked in?

Uncle Monty's sitting room was still pink, and many of the physical features of the house remain, but the range had gone. I'd love to know where it is, and ask for it back, because it belongs to the house and it's a great pity that it's not there.

When working on the renovations, have you had an eye on the film?

I couldn't live with the pink, but wherever anything historic survived, such as cupboards, doors and fire surrounds, even the old plaster ceilings, if they're intact then I've retained them. It was useful having seen the house recorded in film, for example I knew that the door that was missing in the sitting room was a four-panelled one.

Was there graffiti all over the house?

The plywood sheets boarding the property were asking for it really. It was probably the best punctuated graffiti I'd ever seen, and it's such a quotable film. Now it's been under renovation, the only place graffiti turns up is one of the outbuildings, which is still covered with plywood, so my newly painted joinery is thankfully graffiti-free, so people are showing respect to the house now.

How much of the house do you recognise from the film?

When Withnail and Marwood come in and light the hurricane lamp and sit in front of the range, that room is more or less unchanged apart from the range not being there. The scullery where they're trying to force the chicken into the kettle, and the sitting room are much as they were in the film. The fireplace and the cupboards either side, and ceiling beams, make it very recognisable.

What are the film showings like at Crow Crag?

It's the highlight of the year at Crow Crag, organised by Picnic Cinema, (part of Eden Arts in Penrith.). When they approached me in 2012, the building works had started and we had electricity, which was useful for a film projection. It's a yearly event and people have come from as far as Australia and the US, but we also get quite a few that are quite local, and have had a lot of fans up from Bristol.

What are your plans for the future of Sleddale Hall?

Before I started work on the renovation it was quite easy to gain entry, and I'm not sure how much United Utilities visited to check on the property. Perhaps as it became derelict people thought no one cared about it, and it was okay to break in and vandalise it. Fortunately, that no longer happens. When the renovation is complete, I want to use it as a holiday let. It will be a comfortably furnished farmhouse, so *Withnail* fans can visit and have a delightful weekend in the country.

SAM BAIN
WRITER

When did you first watch it and what were your thoughts after that initial viewing?

I definitely watched it on a VHS video like most people in my generation, because it kind of came and went at the cinema. I've seen it so many times over the years, probably 10 times, which may be nothing to some but that feels like a lot to me. It's one of those films that was love at first sight for me, its so unique.

How highly does *Withnail* rate for you in terms of British comedies?

I think it's probably up there as number one or two for me as a viewer, as a fan, right up there with *Life of Brian*. Obviously there's a great connection between those two movies with HandMade and George Harrison, there's a lovely continuity there. Those two films for me are where things peak in terms of films that still delight me. *Withnail* has a particular place in my heart because it's such a wonderful piece of writing. *Life of Brian* is too, but it's an ensemble sketch movie as much as anything else, but *Withnail* is such an extraordinary piece of writing.

How much power do you think there is in that script in terms of information for the actors?

I read the screenplay over twenty years ago when I was starting out as a writer. It was fascinating because some scripts are so different from the film, but the *Withnail* script struck me as not being at all different from the film and was written like prose.

In a way it was an unhelpful script to read for me as a screenwriter who doesn't direct, because it clearly didn't need any translation, because Bruce was going to direct it, and it's written in a very specific way. He had a crystal clear vision of the film he was going make, and he managed to carry that through, which is such a huge deal in the making of any movie. Obviously the casting of the actors is inextricably linked to the film, but the script shines like a beacon throughout the whole film.

What do you think modern-day youth audiences will recognise in the film's characters that will resonate with them?

It's that sense of: 'What the fuck am I doing in my life?'

Me and Jesse [Armstrong] consciously borrowed many things from *Withnail* when we were writing *Peep Show*. Being a certain age in your twenties, just having gone through school or uni, or, drama school in the case of characters in the film, and arriving beached and going: 'What's happening? What the fuck now?' That state can last for a long time, and it does end, but while it's happening it feels like it's never going to.

Why is Withnail's trail of self destruction so fascinating?

He's a perfect example of the tragicomic character, because his self obsession and selfishness is initially funny, but becomes tragic. As you see within the film when he throws his best friend under the bus (if you can describe Monty as a bus) destroying his closest relationship through pure selfishness. That really resonates, but also the narcissism and the sense of self obsession, which I think anyone in their twenties can relate to.

Bruce Robinson said he had all the luck in getting the right ingredients together at the right time place and cast…

The amount if luck you need to get all the ingredients, whether it's cost, money, music, your film is an incredibly complex web of people coming together. Luck is an understatement. When getting films made there's only so much you can control, the rest of it is in the hands of the Gods. The one thing you can fight to preserve is your vision. 'This is the film I want to make. This is why I want to say it, and if I start chopping off the corners, what's the point?'

There are lot of times making a film you might be asked to compromise. There are certain things you can compromise on and things you can't. Knowing the difference is crucial, but Bruce Robinson compromised nothing in *Withnail & I*.

How much truth do you feel there is in the film?

It's got truth running through it like a stick of rock. It has that authenticity, it's no secret that it was based on his life experience living with Vivian and friends, and those relationships were very inspiring. When you're writing, especially starting out, there is that doubt that if you write about your own experience, who's going to care? Who's going to relate? I think that the trick is to go as specific, as authentic, and true as you can. That's how people will relate. No film has been made like *Withnail & I* before or since. It has that authenticity and truth, and that's why people love it. You can't try and make something you think people will like, that's fatal.

What for you is the most melancholic aspect of the film?

It's hard to beat that ending. The speech to the wolves in the park because it's the first time in the film that we're really aware that we've seen a character totally alone. Although it's grim, much of the rest of the movie is joyful, and it's got this wonderful bantering friendship, which a lot of men obviously get into. But the end, there's that sense of isolation and the sense that his dreams aren't going to come true. There's something quite brutally sad about that, but also beautiful. An ending like that is so difficult to pull off because endings are hard anyway, but to make a comedy with such a sad ending work so well is miraculous.

How effective do you think the film was in reflecting the different class backgrounds of Withnail and Marwood?

This is definitely something that I liked about the movie and has informed some of the scripts that I've written in my career, because I think class is such a big thing in British comedy in particular, as well as society obviously, and you know, it really works. The idea of that sense of entitlement in that there's lots of free stuff out there if you if you are privileged enough to be able to access it. That really fuels the plot in a very satisfying way.

Also, that element of tragedy about Withnail being someone who, although privileged, that privilege is almost working against him, because it means that he's maybe not going to put the work in or get himself where he needs to be, so yes, it has a lot of resonance.

What do you admire most about the script?

I don't think there's ever been a film I've ever seen with more quotable lines, it's become a cliché to say that, obviously. You could literally spend an hour and a half recalling all the lines, because pretty much every line is quotable. It's got a language of its own. Once you tune into that, it's like a gift that keeps on giving. I don't think there's been a better script for dialogue ever, frankly.

ABOVE: 'There's always time for a drink.' Photo by Murray Close.

PETER HANNAN
CINEMATOGRAPHER

What did you think when you first read the script?

I must admit, I fell in love with it. I could see the movie as I read it. I see everything in images. I expect all cinematographers are the same. What the film looked like was all on the page. Sadly, HandMade's Denis O'Brien didn't see it the same way. He thought it should be a bright and an over-the-top British romp – a Carry On. Bruce didn't see the film that way – nor did I.

What did you think when you first saw Crow Crag?

Excited. Crow Crag became one of the film's characters, a 'Star.'

We were very lucky that we had such a location. When the first day of principal photography arrived, I just could not get to the set quick enough. The shoot was an absolute joy every day.

So, were you there to hear Bruce's speech to the cast and crew on that first day of shooting?

Yes, I remember feeling embarrassed for him at the time. I felt he was apologising before he started, but he did not need to. He was so professional and totally supported by the crew.

THIS PAGE: Peter Hannan and Bruce Robinson discussing the bull scene, filmed at Scarside Farm track.

OPPOSITE TOP: Withnail demands attention, at Haweswater Reservoir. Photo by Murray Close.

OPPOSITE BOTTOM: Director of photography Peter Hannan and Bruce fine-tuning the shot.

What camera film and lenses did you use?

The camera was an Arri BL with Cooke lenses. The film stock was Fuji. We had a weird request by production before shooting that they wanted the frame film aspect ratio to be 1:185 hard mask, which turned out to be an error on their part. The whole camera department had queried this request; but we were told that this request had come from Hollywood.

The sound department were very happy with this request as they could get the sound boom much closer to the actors. In Post, Hollywood enlarged the film to the now old 'TV ratio.' This increased the film grain, but this did not hurt the play.

What was it like working with Bob Smith?

I've done a lot of pictures with Bob, and he excelled on *Withnail*. He got into trouble with Bruce a few times for laughing. Not *really* in trouble, but some stern looks. Bruce didn't want the cast to treat it as a comedy. It had to be performed as a straight

piece as far as they were concerned. Bob couldn't help himself a couple of times.

Sadly, Bob passed away – there aren't many of us crew left. Colin Davidson our Focus Puller, Reg Parsons my Gaffer and Paul Heller the Producer have all gone. Paul was on set a lot. He had a lovely manner. He really looked after Bruce.

How did the arrival of Richard Griffiths change the atmosphere on the set?

I don't think it did. Richard G. was a real player, a true Thespian. He performed his role beautifully. He wasn't playing an over-the-top stereotypical English comic homosexual. His timing was perfect. What incredible lines he was given to deliver – poetry! A great man to work with. I worked with Richard G. again on *Harry Potter* a hundred years later.

How did you approach the opening credits?

My attitude to the whole film was low-key and gritty. I think the only time I got anywhere near high-key was in the cafe – with the fried egg sandwich.

How pleased were you with the 'I'm going to be a star' scene, and how it was set up?

It was truly pouring – absolutely pissing it down. We were so lucky to get that iconic shot of Richard E. It was shot right at the end of the day – we had little daylight left. The silhouette of Withnail walking across the horizon was by the skin of our teeth.

We could not have gone for another take – it would have been night. There was one big cloud that could have been a bit higher, and that would have been magic. That was the moment: if we didn't shoot it, we wouldn't have got it.

What was it like working with Paul McGann and Richard E. Grant as leads?

Easy. Paul came from an acting dynasty. Richard E. was coming out of left-field, but Bruce had rehearsed the scenes so well it always worked. Both Paul and Richard E. had characters that were so well drawn. Reading the script felt like you were watching the film, and I've never felt like that so much with any other script.

Would you discuss each scene in detail with Bruce before you shot it?

No. If Bruce had ever said: 'I don't like this shot,' we'd have discussed what he wanted. But I don't remember ever having that discussion. The size of the sets limited choice, but helped the story. Sometimes I couldn't get a light where I wanted, but they were always very happy difficulties. Nic Roeg would say: 'Use the difficulty.'

Did you ever consider that most aspects of the film were being seen through Marwood's eyes?

The camera never really approached it that way. Although there are more long shots of Richard by himself than there are of Paul as Marwood.

The colour palette was fairly subdued. It almost seemed like a black and white film on occasions. How did you get that feel?

I liked that. There were a few discussions with the Art Department about the palette, but again it was following the script. It would have been wrong to have bright, primary colours. It just would not have worked. The bathroom was primary; the exception that makes the rule. We were lucky we had such rotten weather, which helped as well. The subdued palates ran through everything.

What was your favourite scene in terms of the lighting?

Probably Paul getting up from the chair in the opening scene. It set up the movie.

What did you think when you first saw _Withnail_ at the cinema?

Pleased. I had had lots of phone calls from people who had seen previews beforehand, saying how wonderful it was. So I had more than an inkling it worked. It didn't take off immediately, but it was a classic sleeper. A slow burner. It's still burning.

Can you tell us how it came about you worked on that restoration edition in 2014, and how different was the overall look of that edition that you helped create?

Initially by a New York company called Criterion. I did not want to rephotograph the film. To me, its look was part of it. I had two and a half days to remaster from a print. The Company gave me a Videodisc copy. It looks like an old LP, which is on my wall.

Some years later for a new release, Arrow Films gave me three days for another restoration with a very good colourist. This time from the neg, which was so much better to work with. Overall, the restoration was just a little bit of this and a little bit of that.

Do you have a favourite personal scene?

No, because if I pick one, I'll be leaving another out, and they were all so special.

What are your thoughts on _Withnail_ thirty-five years on?

I'm so lucky and so proud to have been a part of it. My son, when he was at Bristol University in the late '90s was lighting a play : _Glengarry Glen Ross_ at the theatre, and asked me to go down and watch it. Doing the right thing as a father, I suggested we went for dinner afterwards, and he asked if he could bring a mate. I said of course, and he ended up bringing about 10 people – the whole cast and crew. I asked if anyone would like a drink? One of them said: 'We want the finest wines available to humanity,

we want them here and we want them now.' They didn't know I'd worked on it.

They all started quoting _Withnail_ lines one after the other. My son said to them: 'Pete had something to do with that movie.' They asked what I did, and my son said the Director of Photography. They all gathered around my chair and knelt before me and chanted: 'We're not worthy' It was extraordinary – a good 15-plus years after the movie had been released.

Every now and then in pubs and restaurants, I hear quotes from the film from people of all ages. It always makes me smile.

How unique is Bruce Robinson as a director?

I've worked with some brilliant directors in my time, but he's special in so many ways. His players are well rehearsed, he doesn't get cross – doesn't scream and shout at all – ever. I did _How to get Ahead in Advertising_ with him as well. He was the same. An absolute special person, a joy to be with. A pleasure and an honour to have been part of his crew on these two films.

ABOVE: Standing behind this wall was considered safe until the bull ran through it.

STEVE DOHERTY
COMEDY PRODUCER

I think I was born to love *Withnail & I.* As with the film, my life story started in September 1969, took shape but was largely ignored in the 1980s, and then gained a small but enthusiastic following in the 1990s. It even involved a brief holiday in the north country but more of that later.

Like all good cults, *Withnail* involved an enthusiastic introduction from a friend and I didn't quite understand it on first exposure; the fetid kitchen, the fear, that fried egg sandwich. 'Why do you like it so much? There's not much of a story', I asked the chap whose VHS copy was already tatty from repeated screenings. Then I started to listen as the rhythm of the dialogue carried me up the M6 to Crow Crag, through the rain. Then my own clouds lifted and I stood (thankfully not in my underpants) surrounded by majesty.

And that's when it becomes part of your life, especially when you share a flat with another fan of the film, in front of whom you can never eat soup ('Why didn't I get any soup?') never suggest a new venture ('it's impossible, I've looked into it') and never attempt *anything* without the gloves. I'm not the first and won't be the last to revel in the beauty of Robinson's dialogue, but I understand and appreciate the influence that it has had upon my own work (I make comedy for radio and TV) where I want all the scripts to sing like Bruce's. Some do … some don't.

Let's face it, if you've watched the film you'll know that nothing really happens; two unlikely friends take an ill-advised trip to the English countryside, their benefactor reveals an ulterior motive and they go home. Yes, other stuff happens: cake and wine, fuel and wood, a leg bound in polythene… but what I'm glued to is not the story but the people. As much as I am in turns revolted, terrified and intimidated by them, I am beguiled by their words and want them to never stop talking. One extraordinary character after another after another, each representing a particular kind of *Englishness* at a very particular time in English history, dreamed up and made real by one remarkable man's creative vision.

I had the incredibly good fortune to be introduced to Bruce Robinson once. It was brief but it was meaningful. To me, at least. I was at Hay Festival in mid-Wales (not far, it turned out, from where Mr R. now lives in tranquil semi-retirement), when I saw someone I vaguely knew standing with someone I wish I did. 'Fuck me. That's Bruce Robinson!', I said to my wife. My line of work means that I periodically get to spend time with well-known people; writers, actors – not so much 'Hello' magazine as the middle pages of 'The Observer'. My point of view has always been 'they're just people' and speaking to people isn't hard, so I straightened my jumper and went over. The cliché is 'don't meet your heroes'. Well, the cliché is wrong; he was *exactly* as charming-if-disarmingly-vague as I could ever have hoped him to be. It's five minutes I'll never forget. I can't say the same for him.

Such was my naïve devotion to the film in the pre-internet early '90s that I decided I would undertake a solo pilgrimage to the Lakes and indulge my inner Marwood with a slice of Victoria sponge in the Penrith Tea Rooms. With or without the approval of Miss Blennerhassett. I hired a car whose empty screen wash bottle made a particularly filthy evening on the M6 almost as perilous as that of my heroes. It's not a big town and I told myself that I was sure I'd find the filming location as I drove around for half an hour. I even got out and walked about. I was quite struck by how unlike that in the film this town seemed to be. And for good reason: those scenes were filmed in Stony Stratford, Buckinghamshire. I had literally come on holiday by mistake.

I watched *Withnail & I* again before writing this. Of course I did. I'm not one for arch metaphorical interpretations as a rule, but it struck me that in 2022 we might just be at the end of another era. 'Shat on by Tories, shovelled up by Labour.' We can only hope! In the meantime, thank you Bruce; mine's a fried egg sandwich.

DONAL LOGUE

ACTOR, PRODUCER, WRITER

I remember my girlfriend, Caitlin, and I walking around Baker Street one cold afternoon looking to kill time. Passing a movie theatre, she stopped and said: 'Ooh, this looks interesting.' She was standing in front of a poster for a new film called '*Withnail & I.*'

At first glance, I was unsure of what to think. The poster art (by Ralph Steadman) suggested something zany, which, in my experience, doesn't always mean good. While I think Ralph Steadman's art is fantastic (as well as Hunter S. Thompson's writing – something Steadman has become deeply associated with) I suspected the film might be something that was trying to sell a world of gonzo-style wackiness without any depth. I couldn't have been more wrong.

Nothing better to do, we bought tickets and settled into a remarkably empty theatre. The first few minutes into the movie, I still had doubts. A film about drug-addicted, alcoholic, out-of-work actors? Few movies about actors have ever worked. The subject matter can be thin, self-absorbed stuff (and I say this as a self-absorbed, alcoholic actor) – and something actors who want to write screenplays are cautioned against doing. But, almost immediately, the cleverness of the dialogue and the strength of the Paul McGann and Richard E. Grant's performances broke any misconceptions I carried into the theatre.

The first thing that stood out was that almost every single line in the film was quotable, but never in a way that slowed the momentum of the story. The combination of the dialogue and the level of commitment of the actors was so deep from the jump, the comedy so precise, Caitlin and I found ourselves howling in the cinema. And then the story shifted. While the introductory scene of Withnail's uncle (played by the late, great Richard Griffiths) was laugh-out-loud funny, a layer of pathos was added to the film that would become the foundation the story rested on. I realised the power of *Withnail & I* wasn't in

the insanely brilliant one-liners and quirky characters, it was in its sadness.

Years ago, a young screenwriter crossed paths with the legendary Billy Wilder walking across the Paramount lot. Billy asked him, 'What are you working on? The young man said, 'A love story.' Without breaking stride, Wilder asked: 'What keeps 'em apart, kid?' 'What keeps them apart? is the question at the heart of *Withnail & I*, which is a film about unrequited love with (especially in the novel) the most tragic of outcomes. We left the picture-house and walked back to Regent's Park where Caitlin was living while doing a semester abroad programme. We walked by the Regent's Park Zoo where Richard E. Grant delivered the famous *Hamlet* monologue from at the film's end – a conclusion that was both surprising and inevitable and incomparably beautiful in construction. Bruce Robinson hadn't hijacked Shakespeare, he'd interpreted him in thrilling way. I couldn't shake the film and returned for a second viewing that same night. Passing the poster for the second time, I thought 'O ye of little faith.' The poster art was forgiven – if the zaniness and comic brilliance got them in the seats, it would be the heart of the story that kept the audience wanting to come back again and again. I was lucky to have lived in England when *Withnail & I* came out and became a big vocal proponent for the film to my friends in the States when I returned home. As it wasn't available on VHS, those of us who had seen it became a special club. One of my first bonding experiences with a young Paul Rudd, before he'd started his career, was over our shared love for the film. When it became available on video, we even did an interview in *Interview* magazine about why we loved it so much. And we got it, the way so many others did. While *Withnail & I* is perhaps the most quotable comedy of all time, what makes it an enduring classic is the sadness at its heart.

ACKNOWLEDGEMENTS

Heartfelt gratitude and thanks to Bruce Robinson for getting involved, inspiring the book, the entertaining interviews, and inviting me up to scan the memorabilia. The sky was beginning to bruise, and I'm grateful I was not forced to camp. This book wouldn't have happened without Bruce's approval and it's been an absolute joy working with him.

A big thank you to Bruce's wife Sophie for her hospitality and the kind use of her amazing behind the scenes photos.

A special thanks to all the cast and crew interviewees who shared their memories and were so generous with their time and energy- it meant everything to the project.

Cast: Richard E. Grant, Paul McGann, Ralph Brown, Daragh O'Malley, Tony Wise and Michael Wardle.

Crew: Peter Hannan, Peter Frampton, Sue love, Matthew Binns, and Murray Close.

Music: David Dundas, and Rick Wentworth.

Many thanks to the publishing team at Titan. Especially to Frank Gallaugher, the finest acquisitions editor known to humanity, and Emil Fortune, our brilliant editor. Many thanks to both for buying into the concept.

Many thanks for the superb design work by Martin Stiff.

Much appreciated the wise advice from my agent Mal Peachey at Essential Works.

Martin Keady deserves special mention for his terrific writing, invaluable assistance and copy editing – chin chin.

A massive thank you for the incredible personal contributions from: Sam Bain, Alistair Barrie, Andrew Birkin, Dean Cameron, Bernard Casey, Margaret Cho, Steve Doherty, Gerard Johnson, Matt Johnson, Martin Kessler, Donal Logue, Diane Morgan, Iain Morris, James Ponsoldt, Paul Tanter, and Paul Webb.

Especial thanks to Charlie Higson for his superb reflection of 'a film that seemed to come from nowhere – *Withnail & I*.'

Deep Gratitude to Murray Close for finding those amazing unseen photos, and kind intros, and to his agent, Luisa Bockmeulen for helping organise Murray's photo licensing.

A big thank you to Andy from McCulloch copy for the sterling job helping with copyediting.

Neil Ferguson you terrible cult – many thanks for the soundtrack piece.

Big thank you to Richard Fleury for fixing up a piece on the Jag one last time.

Deep appreciation to Andrew Birkin for the fascinating interview.

Thanks to Sleddale Hall owner Tim Ellis. 'I know where you are, you're at Crow Crag.'

Many thanks to the Withnail Facebook groups and their followers for their support, endless 'sherries' and constantly asking if I'm published. Yes I am.

Love to my wife Sher, and Phoebe and Ava, and in memory of Lewis and Juanita.

I'd like to pay tribute to Richard Griffiths and all the cast and crew of *Withnail & I* that are no longer with us, and dedicate this book to them, and to Bruce for his exquisite creation.

Chin chin

Toby Benjamin

RIGHT: Final scene clapperboard, August 1986.